I read this book cover to cover i   ..ys—I just couldn't put it down! *Beyon. ~range County* is very inspirational and enlightening. Lydia helped ignite my fire to seek my current purpose! I learned so much about myself through her stories and the scriptures she chose to relate to her experiences.

—Alexis Bellino, *The Real Housewives of Orange County*

Lydia's book really hit home with the struggles I dealt with while being a part of the entertainment business. It is a real and raw depiction of everyday struggles we go through as Christians. She gives great advice founded in Scripture. This is a book I will refer to over and over to help keep me grounded in my own walk with Christ.

—Gretchen Rossi, *The Real Housewives of Orange County*

Beyond Orange County gives us an inside peek into the exciting yet often toxic world of reality TV while bringing home powerful, life-changing truths about walking victoriously with Christ. A must read for anyone who struggles with finding her way in our materialistic, sexualized, media-sapped culture.

—Kim Tapfer, author of *I Am—Transformed in Him* and women's teaching leader at Mariners Church, Irvine, CA

Lydia has written a book for women that is honest and real, speaking to the heart of a woman's life in all its complexities, joys, heartaches, and victories. Candid and refreshingly open, Lydia takes you way beyond the OC by plunging straight into halls of meaning where family and faith are the key and central elements of a life lived well.

—Noelle Cablay, author of *Pieces of Sky: a memoir*

In *Beyond Orange County*, Lydia captivates with her personal stories filled with struggle and conflict in overcoming the allure of fame and fortune. Her stories are real, her vulnerability is real, and her faith is real. This is a must read for anyone struggling with the trappings of fame and fortune, or really anyone for that matter!

—Bob Schrimpf, director of
The Gathering Youth Ministry, La Jolla, CA

Lydia has a genuine heart to live out her faith. In this book she vulnerably tells her story of following Jesus in a way that will inspire others to do the same.

—Phil Wood, pastor of Redemption Church
of Costa Mesa, CA

beyond orange county

A *Housewives* Guide to Faith and Happiness

Lydia McLaughlin

WORTHY®
PUBLISHING

Published by Worthy Books, an imprint of Worthy Publishing Group, a division of Worthy Media, Inc., 134 Franklin Road, Suite 200, Brentwood, Tennessee 37027.

WORTHY is a registered trademark of Worthy Media, Inc.

HELPING PEOPLE EXPERIENCE THE HEART OF GOD

eBook available wherever digital books are sold.

Library of Congress Control Number: 2015930267

Unless otherwise noted, Scripture quotations are taken from THE HOLY BIBLE, NEW INTERNATIONAL VERSION®, NIV® Copyright © 1973, 1978, 1984, 2011 by Biblica, Inc.® Used by permission. All rights reserved worldwide. Scripture quotations marked NASB are taken from NEW AMERICAN STANDARD BIBLE®, Copyright © 1960, 1962, 1963, 1968, 1971, 1972, 1973, 1975, 1977, 1995 by The Lockman Foundation. Used by permission. Scripture quotations marked ESV are taken from The Holy Bible, English Standard Version®, copyright © 2001 by Crossway, a publishing ministry of Good News Publishers. ESV® Text Edition: 2011. The ESV® text has been reproduced in cooperation with and by permission of Good News Publishers. All rights reserved. Scripture quotations marked MSG are taken from The Message. Copyright © 1993, 1994, 1995, 1996, 2000, 2001, 2002. Used by permission of NavPress Publishing Group. Scripture quotations marked NLT are taken from the New Living Translation Holy Bible, copyright© 1996, 2004, 2007, 2013 by Tyndale House Foundation. Used by permission of Tyndale House Publishers Inc., Carol Stream, Illinois 60188. All rights reserved.

Italics added to direct Scripture quotations are the author's emphasis.

Some names and identifying details have been changed to protect the privacy of the individuals involved.

For foreign and subsidiary rights, contact rights@worthypublishing.com

ISBN: 978-1-61795-423-8

Cover Image: Rod Foster
Cover Design: brandnavigation.com
Interior Design and Typesetting: Christopher D. Hudson & Associates, Inc.

Printed in the United States of America
15 16 17 18 19 WOR 8 7 6 5 4 3 2 1

To Doug. You have my heart.

Forever.

Contents

Acknowledgments ix

Charge to You xi

1. Answering the Call.................................. 1

2. A New Reality....................................... 16

3. Dealing with Discouragement................. 26

4. In the Spotlight.................................... 39

5. Moving On 53

6. Burning Bush Moment 65

7. Our Identity.. 78

8. Love, Love, Love 94

9. Family Matters 109

10. Created Beautiful 120

11. Confident Lady 133

12. Forgiveness 145

13. Finding Peace 159

14. In the World, Not of the World 172

15. Live Your Great Adventure 184

Notes 192

Acknowledgments

I WOULD LIKE TO express my gratitude and thanks to the many people who saw me through this book, to all those who provided support and walked with me through this journey.

I am so grateful for the tribe of people who encourage, love, and inspire me. From my Young Life mentors to my grandparents, so many people have left their fingerprints on my heart.

My mother, Judy, is constantly sprinkling the world with fairy dust and demonstrating selfless motherly love daily to me. My father, Scott, always believes and encourages me and ignited my journey of faith. My two brothers, Jesse and Geoff, have taught me so much about the Lord.

Thank you to my mentor, Noelle, who in the desert never wondered why I was building a boat but held the hammer for me.

My heartfelt thanks to Emily, Kristin, Sarah, Christine, Amber, Nicole, Jenny, Jen, Kelly, Brittney,

Nikki, Virginia, Lauren, Amanda, and all my girls who have prayed for me, walked with me, and supported the dream of this book.

I am grateful for my castmates on *The Real Housewives of Orange County*. I would like to thank Bravo, Evolution, and all the people I met during my experience on the show. I am thankful for the friendships with Alexis, Jim, Gretchen, and Slade that continue to grow.

I would like to thank Worthy Publishing, my agent Elissa, my literary agent Mollie, and my amazing editor Jen for making this book a reality.

I would like to shout out to Mackenzie, who made hot cocoa and played endless amounts of LEGOs with my boys so I could focus and get my thoughts down on paper.

I would like to thank my three sons, who have made me into a mom and are my greatest sources of joy and inspiration.

Lastly, my heartfelt love and gratitude to my husband, Doug. You are my rock and anchor. Your support and belief in me has made this book not just a dream but reality. Your pursuit for perfection always pushes me, and you have made me the happiest girl I know. I love doing life with you.

Charge to You

Whatever you are, try to be a good
one.
    —*William Makepeace Thackeray*

M Y FRIEND WENT to hear her favorite author, Jen Hatmaker, speak at a conference where we live, in Orange County, California.[1] Afterward, she shared with me some insights she had learned from the weekend.

Jen had asked the conference attendees to picture Jesus walking on the dusty roads and His disciples walking alongside Him. She invited her listeners to envision Jesus and all the disciples walking from village to village and to imagine how dusty they must have gotten while traveling along dirt roads with only sandals on their feet.

The image in your mind reminds us of what our walks with Jesus should be like. We want to follow Jesus so closely that the dust from His feet is all over us.

That is what I desire, because that is what real living is all about. And that is my prayer for each of you as you read this book. I pray that these words will point you to the road where Jesus is walking and that the dust from His sandals would radiate onto you because you are walking so closely with Him, wherever He should lead you.

Answering the Call

Will you be the master of your life
or will you hand your life over to
the Master?
—*Craig Clarke*

M Y HUSBAND, DOUG, and I have been married for
nine years and we have three precious little boys.
When I was pregnant with our oldest son, Stirling, Doug
and I decided to open an art gallery in Laguna Beach.
Just what all first-time parents need, a new business adventure, right? We spent my pregnancy marveling at my
expanding belly and our growing baby's every kick, along
with remodeling and working on our art gallery.

After months of hard work and preparation, it was finally the night of the opening party for our gallery, Skylab Modern Art. Many people came to the party to celebrate with us, including several local newspaper reporters who were there to cover the new art gallery opening in town. We had planned this party for months and had done advance photo shoots for all the Laguna Beach newspapers.

As I was setting down the food for the party, I felt my first real contraction. I had been feeling minor contractions all day, but I had figured it was just because I was on my feet working hard for our gallery opening. This contraction was different. It was a very clear sign: *Mom, I am coming now. Let's do this thing called birth!*

I calmly walked over to Doug and told him I was in labor. Isn't it funny how God works? He has perfect timing and has everything planned out—no accidents. Doug and I left our gallery opening party in the trusted hands of Doug's brother Marshall, and we went to the hospital. The story of my going into labor on opening night of our art gallery ended up making it into the article of a local newspaper. The reporter wrote that we gave birth that night not just to our first child but also to our new business.[1]

As the fog of sleepless nights and adjusting to life with a baby gradually wore off, Doug and I really invested in our new business venture of being art gallery owners. We met all kinds of artists and designers and photographers. We found ourselves in this cool world of artistic people. It was there that we were approached by our now business partner to start a magazine.

First Connections to Hollywood

Our friend Mark had a vision for a magazine that would celebrate the triumph of the human spirit. Mark's family is well connected in Hollywood—his grandfather produced the television classics *I Love Lucy* and *The Dick Van Dyke Show*. With Mark's Hollywood connections and our connections with photographers and designers, we decided to partner together, work hard, and create a magazine.

The result was the launch of *Beverly Hills Lifestyle* magazine. We have learned so much during the past six years of publication, and the magazine has taken us on journeys to places, both professionally and personally, we could never have imagined. As I pursue a relationship with the Lord longer and longer, I see that is oftentimes how He works. Doug and I had a plan for our lives—with our own goals, dreams, and aspirations—though we didn't have a specific, step-by-step plan. And even if we did, it wouldn't have been as interesting as the life we were living!

As our magazine increased in circulation and became more influential in the Beverly Hills area, a whole new reality was about to be opened to us as well.

Beverly Hills Lifestyle magazine has many contributors for every issue. Some people contribute to just one issue, while others partner with us to write an article for every issue. One of the contributors Mark brought to the magazine was his friend Lisa Vanderpump, whom he introduced to us as "Pinky." Pinky has been writing a recurring column for every issue of our magazine since the beginning.

To us, she was not Lisa Vanderpump—the famous woman featured on the reality TV show *The Real Housewives of Beverly Hills*. She was just Pinky, a Beverly Hills socialite who knew the most fabulous spots in Beverly Hills. Pinky wrote about her favorite hair salons and facialists and always wore all pink while holding her dog Giggy for her photo shoots with us. She was an entertaining character and, in our opinion, a perfect choice for a contributor to the magazine.

The Real Housewives of Beverly Hills launched about a year after we met Pinky, and she was a favorite of many who watched the show. Doug and I would watch the show and feel a connection to this far-off world because we knew Pinky—and she was on reality TV! It was fun to have a connection to the glamorous Hollywood world, and it was fascinating to have a somewhat inside view into one of the show's most beloved characters.

The Call That Changed Everything

Two years later, Doug and I had our second son, Maverick. We continued to work on our magazine and art gallery. Then one day I got a phone call that changed everything.

On a sunny Thursday afternoon in 2013, I had just finished working out at a 24 Hour Fitness and was walking out the gym door, on my way to pick up my sons from my mom's house. My cell phone rang, and I looked down to see that the incoming call was from a 310 area code, which is Los Angeles. I figured it was something related to our art gallery or magazine. Since my children weren't with me, I knew there wouldn't be any distracting crying or whining in the background—so it was a perfect time to answer.

The voice on the other end turned out to be a representative from *The Real Housewives of Orange County*. I had not spoken to her before, but she said she had heard about me and told me I'd be "the perfect fit" for her reality TV show.

Doug and I hadn't watched *The Real Housewives of Orange County* in years. The show launched just after I had graduated college and moved to Orange County, so I watched it for a while to enjoy seeing the Housewives eating at the same spots I went to, but that was years ago. I had kept up with *The Real Housewives of Beverly Hills*, but that was only because of Pinky. Oh wait, Pinky . . . That must have been how the producer had heard of me.

I laughed and quickly told the producer, "No, thank you." I told her that I was extremely flattered to have been considered for the show, but I didn't think I was cut out for reality TV. The producer responded graciously, gave me her direct phone number, and told me I could call her anytime if I changed my mind.

That night I told Doug about the random call I had received hours earlier. At first he laughed with me, but then he said in all seriousness, "You should meet with her."

Was he crazy? I had two young children, a magazine, an art gallery, and a household to run. Oh yeah, and I'm a Christian. I even led a Bible study for moms at my church. I had no business being on a reality show like that! Sure, *The Real Housewives of Orange County* was entertaining to watch, but why would I ever choose to be part of such a thing? I remember telling Doug, "I love my life. Why would I want to ruin it by being on a reality TV show?"

Doug encouraged me to think and pray about it. He suggested that maybe this could be a great adventure, a chance to shine my light for Christ in a unique way.

Making the Decision

The next morning I woke up and sat down to study my Bible. At the time I was going through a Bible study on the Old Testament book of Nehemiah. I remember the moment as if it were yesterday. I was sitting at our kitchen table and drinking my morning coffee from my pink Anthropologie mug. I opened my Bible to the book of Nehemiah, looking up the verses for that day's lesson.

If you haven't heard the biblical story of Nehemiah, let me sum it up for you. Nehemiah was a man who was living in the palace of a king. He was basically the king's right-hand man. Out of the blue, God called Nehemiah to go to a foreign land to build a wall. Get his hands dirty. Help people he hadn't met. *Leave his palace.*

Similarly, God was tugging on my heart with an out-of-the-blue call. At that moment, I realized that this opportunity to be on *The Real Housewives of Orange County* had come from the Lord. I knew in my heart of hearts that God was calling me to do the show—I don't know how else to explain it. As I was reading the Scripture verses describing God's call to Nehemiah, I quickly understood that my Bible study lesson that morning wasn't a coincidence but divine timing. I had gotten the phone call the day before to step out of my comfort zone and go into a "foreign land," to "get my hands dirty" by joining the world of reality TV, and to help people I had not yet met by shining the light of Christ through the show. And now I was reading Scripture verses about a man who was also called out of his palace to serve the Lord in a very unconventional way. Sometimes God is subtle, and other times He is extremely blatant about what He wants to communicate to us!

I called the producer the next day and expressed my interest, coupled with apprehension. She set up an on-camera interview for me, followed by a meeting with the show's executive producers. When meeting with producers, I think most girls are trying to earn a spot on the show, explaining why they are the perfect fit to be the next Housewife. However, I did the opposite. I told the producers that I wasn't sure about being on the show. I told them I was a Christian and admitted I was nervous that they would try to show contradictions between my behavior and my faith. I honestly told them my fears. They assured me they just wanted me to be myself.

God's Call to a Great Adventure

Our journey with Christ is a call and a great adventure. If we are spending time in the Word and are nurturing our relationship with Him, He will give us clarity about what we should do and where we should go. In John 10:27, Jesus says, "My sheep listen to my voice; I know them, and they follow me." As I prayed about whether to participate in the show, I began to feel a strong peace that this opportunity had come from God, and I knew He was calling me to do it.

Our God is a God of truth and love. He guides us through His Holy Spirit. The Bible tells us, "God is not a God of confusion but of peace" (1 Corinthians 14:33 NASB). Throughout my decision process I was sometimes scared and conflicted, but ultimately I had a clear conviction in my heart. I think many times we know what God is calling us to do; we just have to ask God to give us the courage to take the first, bold leap of faith.

My mentor once compared following God's call on our lives to the biblical story of Noah. Noah spent many years building the ark, even though the world hadn't yet seen rain. He was in a desert building a huge boat, and with every year that passed, I'm sure the people around him shook their heads and laughed at him. But Noah was given a task and he chose to obey God's call, even if it didn't make sense to the people around him. He stayed focused. Noah needed to be surrounded by people who, although they might not have understood why he was building a boat, would support Noah and pass him a hammer.

As I was wrestling with my decision about whether to be on *The Real Housewives of Orange County*, I sought wise advice from people I admire and love. I prayed and asked my friends to pray for me. I spoke with several pastors and Bible teachers I had grown close to.

The idea of my joining the cast of a reality TV show was met with both support and disapproval from family members and dear friends. People in my life were concerned for my family and me. Choosing to be on the show would be a leap of faith. Ultimately the decision was one that I alone would have to make, but I had input from people who ran the gamut from naysayers to supporters.

After listening to their opinions and praying with Doug and others, I knew God had spoken to me and called me to do the show. Although I knew it would be unconventional, I realized that taking the leap of faith to sign up for this reality TV show would be a kind of ministry—a ministry that God had called me specifically to do.

Taking the Step of Faith

Genesis 12:1–2 gives another example of God's unique call on a person's life. In this passage, God says to Abraham, "Go from your country, your people and your father's household to the land I will show you. I will make you into a great nation, and I will bless you; I will make your name great, and you will be a blessing."

Like Abraham, we worship a good God who loves us. He wants to bless us and for us to be a blessing to others. However, His call on our lives can be scary or make no sense. Following God isn't necessarily all rainbows and butterflies, as we are not in heaven yet. God called Abraham to leave his country, to leave his people, and to leave his family. And where was he to go? To a land that God would show him. In other words, Abraham had no idea! He had to obey God by leaving everything he had ever known and going to a place he had never seen. That is a bold call to have on your life!

We have the same promise of blessing set before us now. Yet we often find it so hard to reach for the life God is calling each one of us to experience.

God is calling us on a great adventure. His call is unique and personal and specific to each of us and our talents and gifts. Many times this calling requires us to go out of the palace like Nehemiah, or out of our country like Abraham, and into a foreign land that God will show us.

How has God called you in the past? Have you answered His calling, or have you stayed in the comfort zone of your country and missed out on a great adventure? Is God calling you to do something now? Be bold, friends! Even if it doesn't make sense or you don't know what the next one hundred steps are, take the first step of faith today.

Created for Something Special

When Doug and I decided to sign on for the eighth season of *The Real Housewives of Orange County*, we pretty much hit the ground running. The experience was kind of like having our first baby. I remember leaving the hospital with newborn Stirling. Doug and I loaded our precious bundle of joy into the car and drove out of the hospital parking lot. We looked back to see if the nurses were still watching us leave. We couldn't believe they were allowing us to take home this tiny, helpless newborn baby without any supervision or a handbook!

Doug and I had a similar feeling when we decided to be part of the show. The crew showed up at our home, put a mic on each of us, and suddenly we were thrown into the reality-TV world. I guess that's what makes the video footage raw and real—no one explains to you what to expect or how to act. We thought it was unbelievable that there wasn't a handbook or any supervision!

God created each of us with a specific plan and purpose. He created you for something special and wants the world to see Christ through you in a unique way that only you can shine. During that time in my life, I felt called to shine my light for Christ through a reality TV show. Some may call that bizarre and crazy, and maybe they are right. That seems to be how Jesus likes to do things, though.

I pray that each of us would be a light to the world. We all long to matter and to have our lives mean something. That longing is there for a reason. God placed in our hearts a passion for more to ignite our boldness to follow Jesus, wherever He is calling us.

I have no clue what God's call is in your life, but I know He has one for you. He has a specific plan for you—a unique calling specifically for you. All He usually shows you is the first step. Walk in faith and answer God's call by taking that first step, friends—and you will begin your own great adventure!

Discussion Guide

- Describe a time when you had an experience similar to Lydia's call to leave the "palace" and follow God's call on her life.

- Romans 10:17 says we can hear Christ through His Word: "So faith comes from hearing, and hearing through the word of Christ" (ESV). Have you ever sensed God speaking to you through His Word? If so, how did that experience strengthen your faith?

- Answer these questions, posed in the chapter: How has God called you in the past? Have you answered His calling, or have you stayed in the comfort zone of your country and missed out on a great adventure? Is God calling you to do something now?

- What step of faith will you commit to take, right now, to start following God's call on your life and begin your own great adventure?

- Are you ready to commit yourself to learning the biblical principles in this book? If so, consider writing out a commitment or contacting a friend to tell her about your commitment and ask her to hold you accountable to finish this book.

two

A New Reality

Too many of us are not living our dreams because we are living our fears.

—*Les Brown*

I HAD JUST SIGNED on to be the newest cast member of *The Real Housewives of Orange County* season 8, and I had absolutely no idea what to expect. I knew what the show was about, and I knew who some of the Housewives were, but there is no class you can take or book you can read to prepare you to be part of a reality TV show. You kind of just get thrown into the fire and see whether you dance or get burned.

I remember putting my boys to sleep the night before my first day of filming. I was anxious and filled with fear, excitement, and nerves. The kids and I had finished our normal nighttime routine: we read two bedtime books, and then I lie down with them for a while until they doze off so I know they won't be up all night laughing and chatting. Usually I play Solitaire on my iPhone or browse Facebook and Instagram while I wait for the kids to fall asleep.

That night I was scrolling through Facebook and noticed that my friend had posted a video of a commencement speech Jim Carrey had given. Jim Carrey is Canadian, as am I, and so we usually stick together! I glanced at Stirling and Maverick and saw they were both asleep, so I turned down the volume so it wouldn't wake them and listened to the speech.

Jim Carrey spoke to me. Yep, I said it. God used these words from the star of *Ace Ventura*, *The Cable Guy*, and *The Truman Show* to lighten my spirit and put my nerves into perspective. God uses many things in life to inspire us. Often He transforms the everyday stuff of this world into a beacon of light for our adventure with Him. God can encourage us by a church service or by a sunset, through His Word or through a friend. Something doesn't have to be labeled "Christian" to be used by Christ. Truth is truth, and as long as what inspires us lines up with Christ and His Word, then it is good. In my case, God decided to use Jim Carrey's words to give me "the peace of God, which transcends all understanding" (Philippians 4:7).

In this commencement speech, Jim Carrey encouraged the graduating class to follow their dreams. He used his success as an actor as an example that dreams can and do come true. Jim shared a story of his own father, who could have been a great comedian but thought that was too risky a job choice for a man with a family, so he became an accountant instead. He thought it was a safe job, a safe decision. When Jim was young, his dad got laid off from his job as an accountant. His family went through a really hard couple of years, and Jim learned that you can fail at what you don't desire, so you might as well take a chance and follow your dreams.

Now, don't misunderstand—it has never been my heart's desire to be a reality TV star! However, it is my desire to lead women to Christ. It has long been my dream to write a book. I want to use my gifts and talents to point ladies to Christ. I saw this opportunity to be on a hit reality TV show as a chance to go for it! God was giving me a chance to be bold and know that even though I might fail, at least I tried.

That night, I felt encouraged and filled with peace to begin filming the show the next day. I had been sure it would be a sleepless night of tossing and turning, but I slept like a baby knowing and clinging to the promise of Philippians 1:6: "He who began a good work in you will carry it on to completion until the day of Christ Jesus."

I knew that God had started something in me and He wasn't going to abandon me but would carry His call on my life to completion, because that is what He promised in His Word. I slept like a baby because I knew I was in the arms of Christ. And so are you, friends.

God wants to use you and for you to follow Him boldly. He wants you to be His hands and His face to this world, to this generation today, right now. What are your talents? What are your gifts? What are your deepest desires? What makes you full of joy and laughter? What do you love to do? Know who you are, what your passions are, and then shine your light for Christ using those talents. There is only one you!

A Mission to Shine God's Light

As we filmed, I continued to have the mentality that God had called me to be on the show. I knew it was no mistake that I was there, and I saw myself on a mission to shine the light of Christ to my castmates, the producers and crew, and the audience.

Before walking out to film the show, I would often sit in my car with my Bible and read the words of Ephesians 6:10–18:

Finally, be strong in the Lord and in his mighty power. Put on the full armor of God, so that you can take your stand against the devil's schemes. For our struggle is not against flesh and blood, but against the rulers, against the authorities, against the powers of this dark world and against the spiritual forces of evil in the heavenly realms. Therefore put on the full armor of God, so that when the day of evil comes, you may be able to stand your ground, and after you have done everything, to stand. Stand firm then, with the belt of truth buckled around your waist, with the breastplate of righteousness in place, and with your feet fitted with the readiness that comes from the a new reality

gospel of peace. In addition to all this, take up the shield of faith, with which you can extinguish all the flaming arrows of the evil one. Take the helmet of salvation and the sword of the Spirit, which is the word of God.

And pray in the Spirit on all occasions with all kinds of prayers and requests. With this in mind, be alert and always keep on praying for all the Lord's people.

After I read those verses, I would remind myself that I was there on a mission and I could rest in the Lord's mighty power. This gave me a sense of strength in my weakness. Many of the Lord's promises that I had read about in the Bible were showing up in my life.

I believe that is what happens when we step out of the ordinary. When we jump out in faith to obey His call, we give Christ the opportunity to catch us. When God is all we have to rely on, He will work in our lives in supernatural ways.

Wherever God has you, you are there for a reason—today, right now. Your circumstances are all part of His divine plan. Scripture says that we are called to be "Christ's ambassadors, as though God were making his appeal

21

through us" (2 Corinthians 5:20). We are how the world will see Jesus. We are making God's appeal to the watching world through our voices, our actions, and our prayers.

Think about that beautiful concept for a moment. We know that we are fighting a battle that is spiritual. We know that God equips us through His Word and truth. We know that He wants us to be His ambassadors to the world. If you are someone who is very familiar with the Bible, please don't let your familiarity with these verses prevent you from experiencing their mighty power.

Letting God Use You

I believe we can live for God no matter where we are. God can and will use us. That is His desire, His plan. God is not just the Lord of churches and holy people; He is the Lord of this whole world. He is everywhere.

Psalm 139:7–12 tells us:

Where can I go from your Spirit? Where can I flee from your presence? If I go up to the heavens, you are there; if I make my bed in the depths, you are there. If I rise on the wings of the dawn, if I settle on the far side of the sea, even there your hand will guide me, your right hand will hold me fast. If I say, "Surely the darkness will hide me and the light become night around me," even the darkness will not be dark to you; the night will shine like the day, for darkness is as light to you.

God can use you right where you are, just as you are. You are a mother? Great. He wants to use you in that role. You are a student? Awesome. He is putting people in your life you could bear witness to. You are shy? That is wonderful. He wants to use you! There is no excuse or perfect time. Wherever you are, whatever you have planned today, let God use you.

Really, what are we so afraid of? As followers of Christ we know that this world is temporary. We believe that we were created for something more. We shouldn't be dictated by fear. We should be guided by faith in Jesus, knowing that it is Him we are here to magnify and portray. He will provide our daily bread (Matthew 6:11). It is for His glory that we take each breath.

I chose to be on a secular reality TV show for Jesus. That doesn't make any sense whatsoever, right? Some of my close friends and leaders of my church didn't understand my calling. I believe they were coming from a place of love and wanting to protect me, but I still had an assurance of God's calling in my heart. I had a clear sense of mission in my mind, so I put the belt of truth around my waist and walked into an unlikely calling.

God can and will use you, too, friends. You just have to take the leap of faith and know He will be there with you every step of the way.

Deuteronomy 31:6 urges us, "Be strong and courageous. Do not be afraid or terrified because of them, for the LORD your God goes with you; he will never leave you nor forsake you."

Discussion Guide

- Can you think of a time when you made a decision based on fear? What happened as a result? Can you think of a time you made a decision based on love? In what ways were the results of your love-based decision different than your fear-based one?

- Have you jumped out in faith in your life right now? If so, how have you seen Christ show up?

- Read Ephesians 6:10–18. How does this passage inspire you to step out in faith and follow God's call?

- As a Christian, do you tend to seek God only during overtly "Christian" times (church services, Bible studies, etc.), or are you always open to hear from God? What are some of the things God uses to inspire or speak to you? How are you actively seeking opportunities for God to talk to you?

- Read Psalm 139:7–12 again. Can you think of a time where you felt like God abandoned you? How did that make you feel?

- Do you want to be bold and used by God in your daily life? Ask God to use you boldly, starting today.

three

Dealing with Discouragement

You'll never find rainbows if you're
looking down.
—*Charlie Chaplin*

WHEN I INITIALLY signed on to do *The Real Housewives of Orange County*, I was very optimistic. I come from a loving and supportive family. They instilled in me a lot of confidence and self-worth. I sort of had the mind-set, *Everyone is going to love me! I am sweet and nice. How could anyone not like me?*

I also surround myself with very positive people. Most of my friends love their husbands, have thriving marriages, and enjoy being moms. There isn't a lot of complaining in my circle of friends. We all like to have a good time and celebrate life together. Of course we have been through our share of heartaches, illnesses, and struggles. Our lives are far from perfect. However, we are friends who love and support one another in a community that is grounded in Jesus.

When life hits us with challenges, we pray for, support, and come alongside one another. There isn't a lot of competition or petty gossip among my girlfriends, as we all love each other and see one another as family. I am so grateful for my friends, and I treasure them dearly. I think being plugged in to a community of believers is an important part of walking with Christ.

Disheartened by the Drama

While we were filming our reunion episode, there was a moment where Vicki and her daughter were going at each other over Vicki's boyfriend, Brooks. I remember sitting on the couch, having nothing to do with the conflict or the drama but feeling so sad. I thought, *How did I end up here? I can't believe I am watching people I know and have grown close to argue. I know this is entertainment, but this is not entertainment to me anymore. I am invested and it is real.*

I sensed the Holy Spirit inside me saying, *You don't have to be here.* So I stood up and walked off the set. I burst into tears as soon as I was out of the cameras' view. No one was attacking me. I wasn't crying because I was personally upset; I was full of sorrow for the brokenness in the room. The drama that was transpiring the moment I left the scene was solely between Vicki and her daughter, but I felt empathy for them. They were having real, deep-rooted family drama, and it was being presented to an audience as entertainment.

I experienced an emotional release when I cried in the hallway. There are no words to describe how intense the filming process is. When people watch the show in their living rooms, they think it is just a TV show so they can have opinions about the "characters." But when you are living out the drama every day, you realize that the people on the show are real people with real problems and real emotions. These are their real lives that are being broadcast for the world to judge and comment on and be entertained by.

I am not complaining, and I knew what I signed up for. But it still hurt. The drama and pain on set still affected me. I wasn't immune to it. It was hard.

A Call That's Not Always Easy

When God calls us out to far-off places, that doesn't mean our journey is going to be easy. Remember the example we read earlier of Abraham being called to leave his country and his family? Think about how lonely and daunting that must have been for him. Following God's call to a far-off place must have been scary and difficult and full of moments of doubt for Abraham. I know because that was how I felt.

I was confident that God had called me to do the show, but it was still hard. God's call is not always easy. Jesus says in Luke 14:27, "Whoever does not carry their cross and follow me cannot be my disciple." To bear a cross is not an easy load. Each of our crosses is different, yet that is the mark of a true disciple. I believe if you ask someone you admire in the faith about her spiritual adventure, she will have stories of grand and blissful moments, along with stories of heartache and defeat. All those things are part of a true Christian walk.

We love to be comfortable and free from worry. Look at our homes and garages full of things we may need at a moment's notice. We often spend our whole lives trying to protect ourselves from any sort of harm. We sign up for insurance in case something happens, so we will be covered and won't have to worry about anything. Yet often the hard times in life are where we see Christ clearly. When we need Him. When all we have is Him. When we set our gaze solely upon our Savior and He is the one to pull us up.

Focusing on the Savior

I love the story of Jesus walking on the water while His disciples are scared and shaking in the boat:

Shortly before dawn Jesus went out to them, walking on the lake. When the disciples saw him walking on the lake, they were terrified. "It's a ghost," they said, and cried out in fear.

But Jesus immediately said to them: "Take courage! It is I. Don't be afraid."

"Lord, if it's you," Peter replied, "tell me to come to you on the water."

"Come," he said.

Then Peter got down out of the boat, walked on the water and came toward Jesus. *But when he saw the wind, he was afraid and, beginning to sink, cried out, "Lord, save me!"*

Immediately Jesus reached out his hand and caught him. "You of little faith," he said, "why did you doubt?"

And when they climbed into the boat, the wind died down. Then those who were in the boat worshiped him, saying, "Truly you are the Son of God." (Matthew 14:25–33)

I especially like the boldness of Peter. So many times I feel like Peter. I can picture myself in the boat with my buddies, and suddenly there is a storm around us. We then see Jesus walking on the water, having this great, crazy, wild adventure—and I want to join Him!

In the Bible story Peter says to Jesus, "Tell me to come to You on the water, and I will!" Jesus tells Peter to join Him, so Peter hops out of the boat and it's awesome. He is walking on water! Peter is a regular person like you and me, and here he is walking on water in the middle of a storm. The wind is blowing, and the waves are crashing—but Peter is having a grand adventure.

Then Peter takes his eyes off Jesus. As he looks around and notices the wind and the waves, he grows afraid. He starts to sink. But *immediately* Christ reaches out His hand and catches him. He doesn't wait for Peter to sink deeper. Christ instantly is there for Him.

I love that story so much because I have lived it. I have felt like Peter, walking on the water by doing something amazing for Jesus—and it's awesome! And then I start to see what is actually going on and the craziness of what is happening. I start to focus on the storm of my circumstances, and then I begin to sink. That was how I felt at the end of *The Real Housewives of Orange County*. I was out of the boat and walking with Jesus on the water, but the waves were crashing and skies were stormy, and I started to sink. Immediately, Christ took me in His arms.

An Encouraging Word from God

About a week after we wrapped filming, my church hosted a women's retreat. So my girlfriends rallied me to drive up to Malibu for the weekend to join them. I was a weary soul at this point. I was tired and spent. I had emptied myself out on the show and felt like I had nothing left spiritually inside of me, so I knew I needed a retreat.

But you know how when you are physically and spiritually exhausted, the last thing you want to do is go to church or read your Bible? Even though spending time with God is the only thing your soul really needs, it's the last thing your flesh desires. Well, that was how I felt at this point. Yet I dragged myself to Malibu for this weekend away.

The Saturday night of the retreat a woman named Merrill spoke, and then we had worship. Merrill was the guest speaker for the weekend. She is from South Africa and has a smile that can only be described as inner joy from the Lord. She looks wise and happy. Plus, with her great accent, everything she says just sounds cool.

During worship I couldn't hold back the tears. I felt a release of so much stress I had been holding in for so long, that once the seal was broken it kept flowing out of me.

I was sitting on the floor, crying, which I *never* do in public. However, no one really noticed me because all the other women were focused on their own worship.

All of a sudden I felt within me a strong sense of this message: *Merrill has a word for you.*

Okay, first things first: I don't talk like that. Not that there is anything wrong with the phrase or the concept of "having a word" for someone as a specific message from God, but I wouldn't use that terminology, especially to myself. So naturally, I started arguing with myself.

A "word" for me? What does that even mean? What do I do: go up to her and say, "Hey, Merrill. Nice to meet you. Do you have a word for me?"

I was deep in arguing mode in my own mind, when all of a sudden a real voice filled the conference hall: "You."

Long pause. "I have a word for you."

I looked up, and then I looked behind me. Merrill had interrupted worship and was staring directly at me.

I started shaking. *Listen up, Lydia,* I told myself. *This is going to be one of those once-in-a-lifetime, burning bush–type moments.*

Merrill began to speak prophecy over me. That had never happened to me before. She used the story of Joseph from the Old Testament and described to me how Joseph was kidnapped and ended up in slavery, but she said I should be encouraged and have strength and faith because *he ends up in the palace again one day.*

God knew that I needed Him. He knew I needed something that I could hold on to that would assure me: *I am still with you, Lydia. I have been with you this whole time. I called you on this journey, and I have not left your side.*

God knew exactly what I needed. He knew that His call for me to be on the show, the peace I had held on to when I thought I was crazy for signing on to such an unorthodox ministry, was the call out of the palace. Now He was using this same word, *palace,* spoken from the stage of a conference hall, to remind me that He hadn't abandoned me. Needless to say, I felt encouraged and a renewed sense of my ministry on the show.

God's Presence During Life's Storms

When you are discouraged, go to God and He will refresh you.

When you feel you are sinking and the waves and storms are crashing in on you, call out to God, and His hand will hold you.

My situation didn't change after the women's retreat. My decisions didn't alter. But I gained a fresh perspective that God hadn't abandoned me. I bared my soul to the Lord during worship, and He showed up for me. And He will show up for you. In a personal and special way, God will show up for you if you invite Him to.

We are in love with a God who is personal. His love for us endures forever. His promises are consistent and never changing. He is real and alive and active. Psalm 23:6 says, "Your beauty and love chase after me every day of my life" (MSG). God is chasing after you, beloved!

Every day, every moment, He is involved and active and present in your life. Don't be discouraged. Look around you and see Jesus in your midst, leading you to walk on water.

Discussion Guide

- Lydia discusses the importance of being part of a good community of believers. How would you describe your friends? Do you have a community of believers in your life? If so, identify the group and how often you meet. Is it a formal group like a Bible study, or is it just a group of friends? If you aren't currently part of a group, how could you cultivate or join a community of friends?

- Read Matthew 14:25–33 aloud. Who do you relate to in this story? Do you tend to stay in the boat where it feels safe, or do you tend to take a walk on water toward Jesus? In what ways are you "stepping out of the boat" in your own life right now?

- Lydia shared her story of God speaking to her on the women's retreat. In what ways have you heard God speak to you in your life?

- First Chronicles 16:9 says, "Sing to him, sing praise to him; tell of all his wonderful acts." How do you feel about worship? In what ways has God shown up in your worship times and spoken to you?

- Read Psalm 23. Does this psalm give you encouragement? In what ways have you seen God's faithfulness in your own life?
- Describe some areas of your life in which you feel discouraged right now. How does this chapter help you begin to feel encouraged that God has not left your side?

four

In the Spotlight

Having God's unconditional love doesn't mean you have his unconditional approval.
—Miles McPherson

Once we wrapped filming season 8 of *The Real Housewives of Orange County*, I was thrown into the next phase of the reality TV world—waiting for the show to air. I didn't experience overnight fame. For me, it was a steady, gradual process.

The Bravo Network had announced that the Orange County franchise had a new Housewife, me. This announcement led to the die-hard fans knowing who I was. They had perhaps seen my picture on a *Housewives* blog or even Bravo's website, where my name and photo had been released in an official statement.

A few people would come up to me at the park or mall and say, "You're the new Housewife, right? I knew I recognized you!"

Being recognized by complete strangers was weird but kind of fun. I was beginning to have maybe one or two sightings a week, and the show hadn't even started airing yet! This was nice in many ways as I had time to close my personal social media accounts and open public accounts where I could approve any photo or information posted there for the world to possibly see . . . and comment on. Fame is a jarring experience, but it is exciting at the same time.

Over the following months the show aired, and my life quickly changed from being normal to becoming a "Bravolebrity." (The show airs on the Bravo Network, so they coined this term for their reality TV stars.) I got to walk red carpets. Take pictures with fans. Give autographs. Be famous. I didn't need a bodyguard or anything, but almost anywhere I went people would recognize me.

The Parallel World of Fame

Being famous is like living in a parallel world, because you are still you. Nothing about you has changed, but all of a sudden you walk into a room and people stare. They do double takes. Some get the courage to ask to take a picture with you. This is the weirdest thing for me because I can put my hand on someone's shoulder when posing with her for a picture, and she is so nervous to be meeting me that she is actually trembling.

Some "Bravolebrities" love the fame game. Of course it's flattering and thrilling, but it also is exhausting. A trip anywhere in public means you are going to be stopped. People will want to talk to you and give you their opinions about your life. You will have your photo taken, and that photo will end up on social media where you can read all their friends' opinions of you. People say you have to have thick skin to be famous, but that doesn't even begin to describe the amount of criticism and opinions you have to endure.

I also started to care more about my appearance. I have always loved dressing up and looking cute, but all of a sudden I couldn't have an off day, or even an off moment. When you feel the whole world is staring at you, this weird sense of responsibility overtakes you where you feel like you don't want to disappoint your fans. You want to be "on" and sweet for them, to live up to their expectations of you. Even if your two-year-old is tugging on you to take him to the bathroom, you still want to be smiling and wearing a Housewife-appropriate outfit.

Ephesians 6:12 says, "For our struggle is not against flesh and blood, but against the rulers, against the authorities, against the powers of this dark world and against the spiritual forces of evil in the heavenly realms." This verse would repeatedly pop into my mind during this period of my life. The desire to be noticed and loved and valued is rooted in every one of us. God designed us this way.

I think being famous and recognized bites deep, and if you are not on guard daily, you will be tempted to buy into your own hype. For me, I quickly realized that I didn't have to dress up and be in Housewife attire to go in public. I just needed to be myself, and I was okay with that. I had to take a step back and remember that my worth and identity have nothing to do with my clothes or looks or being on a reality show. I am Jesus' daughter, and He sees me and loves me for who I am—His beloved child and heir to His throne. Nothing I wear or improve in my physical appearance will change that. I also am a mother, and my sons would much rather me play with them at the park than have my nails perfectly done. My husband is in love with me, the true Lydia, not some Housewife version of myself. I had to rest in that and lean into that. The desire to define my worth based on external things is a battle I continue to fight.

Rivers of Living Water

I believe one reason so many Hollywood celebrities lose themselves, turn to drugs, or fight depression and fall into despair is that they are losing the spiritual battle Paul writes about in Ephesians. I have met many famous people, and I would say overwhelmingly many of them are unhappy and dissatisfied. They seem to have it all, yet I often get the sense that something is missing in their lives. They think their worth is based on being recognized by a stranger, but that doesn't satisfy. Fans get their pictures and then walk away. You can't accumulate so much worldly stuff that you no longer need Jesus. So what if a gossip magazine runs your photo in its weekly column? The next week the same magazine will run another issue with someone else's face. Those things don't quench our thirsty soul. Instead, they leave us void and empty.

Jesus declares in John 7:38, "Whoever believes in me, as Scripture has said, rivers of living water will flow from within them." Rivers of living water will flow from within you if you believe in Jesus! Being famous is fun and exhilarating at times, but it doesn't leave you with living water flowing from your soul. Many times my fame left me with the opposite feelings: nervousness, insecurity, pressured to always be perfect, on guard about what people were saying about me.

I did experience "rivers of living water"—not by being famous but by watching God put fans in my path to encourage me. When I was doing the show, I would meet other Christian women at the farmers' market who understood my ministry and affirmed me for being a light for Jesus on the show. I got to speak to teenagers who had been encouraged and inspired by Doug's and my decision to remain virgins until we were married. It wasn't the red carpets that made my soul sing; it was the body of Christ encouraging me and hearing how I had pointed others to Him in some small way.

Taming Our Tongues

Doug and I had a business meeting in Los Angeles, which is not out of the norm for us. At the time the show was about halfway through airing, so I was used to being noticed and stopped to have my photo taken. However, this particular afternoon was on another level. Doug and I walked out of our meeting and discovered that there were paparazzi waiting for us. Some were close and yelling our names, and some were shooting photos from across the street. They started yelling things about our castmates and asking for our opinions about everyone. Right away Proverbs 21:23 popped into my mind: "Those who guard their mouths and their tongues keep themselves from calamity." Doug and I just smiled and walked quickly to our car.

Another day I was at the grocery store with my son Maverick, and the bagger started talking to me as if we were best friends. He gave me his opinions on my castmates and their husbands as if he personally knew us all. It was entertainment for him to gossip about these people because in his mind they are just characters on a TV show; but the truth is, they are real human beings. They have bad days and good days. They get hungry and tired. They are people.

Ephesians 4:29 says, "Do not let any unwholesome talk come out of your mouths, but only what is helpful for building others up according to their needs, that it may benefit those who listen."

Of course, being on a TV show opens you up to criticism and people having an opinion of you. However, I started seeing that this was just a magnified view of what we do as women all the time. We talk about each other for entertainment. We often don't see one another as sisters of Christ but as competition. Why would we want to tear down someone else? What is it in us that can't wait for the girl to leave the room so we can all turn to our friends to talk about her?

I got a front-row seat for this flaw in humanity because of the TV show. But it really caused me to reflect on my own words and attitudes. I am in no way the conqueror of gossip. You most likely only have to watch one episode of season 8 of *The Real Housewives of Orange County* and you will see me commenting on one of the women. But I do this in my real life as well.

The Bible has so many verses about taming our tongues, and they are challenging and encouraging to me. Here are a few of my favorites:

- Whoever keeps his mouth and his tongue keeps himself out of trouble. (Proverbs 21:23 ESV)
- Whoever goes about slandering reveals secrets; therefore do not associate with a simple babbler. (Proverbs 20:19 ESV)
- If anyone thinks he is religious and does not bridle his tongue but deceives his heart, this person's religion is worthless. (James 1:26 ESV)
- The words of a whisperer are like delicious morsels; they go down into the inner parts of the body. (Proverbs 18:8 ESV)
- Keep your tongue from evil and your lips from speaking deceit. (Psalm 34:13 ESV)
- To speak evil of no one, to avoid quarreling, to be gentle, and to show perfect courtesy toward all people. (Titus 3:2 ESV)
- Whoever slanders his neighbor secretly I will destroy. Whoever has a haughty look and an arrogant heart I will not endure. (Psalm 101:5 ESV)
- I tell you, on the day of judgment people will give account for every careless word they speak. (Matthew 12:36 ESV)

- Do not speak evil against one another, brothers. The one who speaks against a brother or judges his brother, speaks evil against the law and judges the law. But if you judge the law, you are not a doer of the law but a judge. (James 4:11 ESV)

These are just a few of the verses warning us to watch what we say. Our words have power! Whether you are speaking about someone you have never met or your best friend, your words are a reflection of the state of your soul. We need to guard what is coming out of our mouths. Jesus says a powerful thing about our words in Luke 6:45: "A good man brings good things out of the good stored up in his heart, and an evil man brings evil things out of the evil stored up in his heart. For the mouth speaks what the heart is full of."

As we pay attention to our words and our attitudes, we will know the state of our souls. We can avoid becoming offended when people critique us, because we know that misery loves company and perhaps what they are so upset about has more to do with them than it does with us. As the saying goes, "Hurt people hurt people."

Restoring Our Focus

Being in the spotlight is all an illusion, in my opinion. It reminds me of the anonymous quote, "Being famous on Instagram is basically the same as being rich in Monopoly." Nothing about it is real. Yes, when you are famous people know who you are, and you may get a good table at the restaurant, but all that is fleeting. Even Madonna wishes it were still 1985 when she was at the height of her celebrity.

As a result of being on *The Real Housewives of Orange County,* I had the opportunity to speak at my church's youth group and share some of my personal story with them. People would ask me questions about my faith, how to join a life group, or which Bible studies I would recommend. I felt I had become a role model in some small way as God took me on a journey I never would have imagined.

Getting to write this book and perhaps winning the right to be heard by you the reader—these are the things that truly matter to me. The cute outfits and admiration from fans will fade, but the people who shared part of their lives with me and listened to my favorite verses, those things not only made the journey worthwhile but were the reason I believe God put me on this journey in the first place.

The same is true with each of our lives. We can become sidetracked and lose focus. The flashing lights of this world can get so bright that we can veer off our path and look for our worth or purpose in things that aren't of value. We need to be on guard. We need to actively seek the Lord and find what He has placed before us today. Each day He has things that He desires us to accomplish.

We must not lose our way, friends. As believers we are to focus not on what is seen but on what is unseen (2 Corinthians 4:18). Many times we get it twisted and put all our focus on Monopoly money when our heavenly Father wants us to be true millionaires with Him in paradise.

Discussion Guide

- In what ways do you try to get recognition? Does the recognition or fame you get satisfy you?

- Ephesians 6:12 says, "For our struggle is not against flesh and blood, but against the rulers, against the authorities, against the powers of this dark world and against the spiritual forces of evil in the heavenly realms." Have you ever experienced a season of life when you felt as if you were struggling in the spiritual realm? How did you overcome it?

- Jesus declares in John 7:38, "Whoever believes in me, as Scripture has said, rivers of living water will flow from within them." What does this statement from Jesus mean to you? Do you think you have "rivers of living water" flowing from within your soul? Can you give any examples?

- How do you feel about the words you use? Are you lifting people up or tearing people down when you speak? Lydia says, "Your words are a reflection of the state of your soul." What would you say the state of your soul is, based on the words you use?

- Which of the verses about taming our tongues spoke to you the most? Read that verse every day this week and be reminded that your words have power.

- What are some of the ways God is using you right now? How have you seen God use your journey to point others to Him?

five

Moving On

> You are never too old to set an-
> other goal or to dream a new
> dream.
> —C. S. Lewis

AFTER ALL THE episodes from season 8 of *The Real Housewives of Orange County* had aired and publicity for the show was over, we finally had some much-needed down time.

During the break, Doug and I decided to take a trip to Italy with my family. It was refreshing to get back to our roots and remember what family is all about. This vacation was a much-needed time of centering myself and escape.

About four days after we returned home, I received news from my agent that I was being asked back for season 9 of the show.

The first time around, I felt my motives for doing the show were to glorify God. My intentions were pure. They were good. I knew beyond a shadow of doubt in my heart that God had called me to do season 8 of the show.

I would need that same strong sense of God's calling again, because my motives for being on the show the second time around were not as pure. I had gotten a taste of fame and recognition, and it was fun. The money the network offers you is enticing. The dresses and makeup and all things girlie were tempting.

A Difficult Decision

As I prayed about the decision, I didn't feel in my heart of hearts that I was called to do another season of the show. If I was being honest with myself, I felt called to walk away. I had wanted to be a light on the show, but now my true motivation for doing the show again was based more on the worldly benefits. I was definitely torn, and this was a red flag.

The decision of whether to sign on for another season of *The Real Housewives of Orange County* was very hard for me to make. I spoke to wise Christian friends to ask for their input. James 1:5 promises us, "If any of you lacks wisdom, you should ask God, who gives generously to all without finding fault, and it will be given to you." So I prayed and prayed and prayed that God would reveal His will to me, and slowly He did. It wasn't the answer I wanted, but I couldn't deny that I was getting an answer. My prayer of clarity was being answered; I was just receiving a no, which was a hard pill to swallow.

Besides the decision to dive into another season of filming, I found myself at a different crossroads in my personal life. Doug and I have always wanted a big family. He comes from five kids. I come from three. We have always wanted three children, and at that point our boys were four and two. It was time to start thinking about having another baby. When the baby bug bites a woman, there is no turning back. All she sees are babies and pregnant bellies everywhere, and her mind won't stop with that obsession until she has a baby of her own in her arms, whether through birth or fostering or adoption. At least, that has been my experience. The baby train had pulled into the station and I wanted another one. Right then.

Doug and I had spent many nights on our trip to Italy talking about having another baby and wondering how the timing of that would work with the show. Doug saw more than anyone the stress that the show had caused me. He also knew the physical toll that pregnancy had taken on me with our first two children, and he knew that if I tried to do the show while pregnant, it would be too big a burden for me to bear. I knew it too. I didn't want to wait on living our own reality because I was on a reality show. I wanted to have a baby so our third child would be close in age to our other children. It seemed absurd to put our lives on hold for a reality show. This was another red flag in my mind.

I also grew up very close to my grandfather. He was a driving force in who I am. He was a brilliant businessman who wrote books, made documentaries, started multimedia companies, and traveled the world. He always inspired me, and I spent my whole life looking up to him. When I picture him now I see his big smile and hear his booming laugh filling the room.

His last name, and my maiden name, is Stirling, and that is what we named our firstborn. My grandfather also was known as a "maverick," which is what we named our second son.

I wouldn't be who I am today without my grandfather's influence on my life. I have countless memories of him. That fall, when filming of season 9 was scheduled to begin, he was extremely sick. He was living in Canada and couldn't get out of bed. Everyone in my family knew he was ill and worried that if he passed away while I was filming, his death would somehow become part of my story on the show. Perhaps cameras would follow me to his funeral, or in some way my family wouldn't get the privacy they wanted and deserved to mourn his passing. This situation was not discussed by the producers of Bravo, but it was a fear my family had made known to me. Because of this, I didn't feel I had the support of my family to do the show. Yet another red flag.

I didn't understand God's plan. Why would He open all these doors and have this amazing opportunity fall into my lap, only to ask me to walk away? He created me and knows me. He knew I would love the dress-up game and all the benefits that came with doing the show. Why was I getting all these red flags? It didn't seem fair to me and made no sense.

When God Shuts a Door

Acts 16 is filled with stories of Paul and Silas as they traveled and proclaimed the story of Jesus to all sorts of lands and people. Verses 6 through 10 talk about Paul's desire to go to Asia and share the gospel. Acts 16:7 says, "They tried to enter Bithynia, but the Spirit of Jesus would not allow them to."

Why wouldn't the Spirit allow them to go into Bithynia? Paul and Silas obviously had good intentions. They wanted to preach the gospel. But God had other plans for them. Sometimes when God shuts a door, whether by telling us to walk away or by shutting the door for us, we have to trust Him and know that we are the clay and He is the Potter.

God usually doesn't show us His whole plan. He sometimes only directs our next step. That's where our faith has to come in.

God was clearly telling me what He wanted me to do, but there was no five-year plan or explanation that came with that still, small voice within. His plan didn't make sense to me and went against my own desires.

Walking Away from the Show

After much prayer, heartache, and late-night discussions with Doug, we decided to walk away from the show. Once we made the final decision and let the cast and crew know, I released a statement through *Us Weekly*.

The next day I was just sad. My agent wanted me to let the dust settle before pursuing any other projects, so I felt all my dreams were put on a shelf to collect dust. The Housewives started filming season 9, and a big part of me wished I was there with the girls—not for good, right, pure, or holy reasons, but for my girlie, ego-driven emotions.

That's the kind of sacrifice we sometimes have to make for following Jesus. I wish I could tell you that making the decision to walk away from the show was easy and void of any pain, but that's not the journey of following Jesus. In Matthew 16:24–26 Jesus says, "If anyone would come after me, let him deny himself and take up his cross and follow me. For whoever would save his life will lose it, but whoever loses his life for my sake will find it. For what will it profit a man if he gains the whole world and forfeits his soul? Or what shall a man give in return for his soul?" (ESV).

Jesus never says that following Him will be easy; He just says it will be worth it. Sometimes following Jesus hurts. We may have to give up that handsome boyfriend we never should have started dating in the first place. We might have to leave the job we are in and pursue our real passion, which can be terrifying. Perhaps we have to sacrifice our time to serve someone who needs our help. Sometimes following Jesus is messy and sacrificial, but if it didn't cost us anything, how would the world ever see our faith? How would our faith be made stronger?

Looking Back

I now sit here a year later, and I am holding our third baby boy! I find myself overflowing with emotion. Yes, I am post-pregnancy and emotional, but also I see God's fingerprints all over this past year. I may not get stopped for photos as often as before, but I have a passion and love for my Savior that I would never trade for any amount of temporal fame. I know Him more intimately and have relied on Him in ways I'd never experienced before. He has shown up and made His presence known in my life again and again. He has blessed my family and me in ways I could never have imagined.

If I had decided to sign on for season 9, who knows what it would have been like filming while being pregnant. I'm grateful I didn't. My grandfather passed away over Christmas 2013, and I would have perhaps had an emotional breakdown from dealing with the sadness and pain of his death while also trying to protect my family's privacy during that time. I truly believe God protected me and shielded me from all of that pain.

I look back and know God intended me to be on *The Real Housewives of Orange County.* The show has opened so many doors and introduced me to so many people. My mind has been blown by the adventures I've gone on due to the show. However, I also know for sure that He called me out of it.

Psalm 40:8 says, "I delight to do your will, O my God; your law is within my heart" (ESV). In making this decision, I needed to put my Father's will above my own. I saw all the red flags and needed to listen to what God was speaking into my heart.

Who is to say what the future holds? Perhaps Doug and I will one day return to reality TV, or even to *The Real Housewives of Orange County.* I never would have thought being a Housewife would have given me the opportunity to write a Christian book filled with Scripture! I also have grown close with Alexis from that experience. She is such a sweet, dear friend and I am grateful she is in my life. During filming I mostly argued with Gretchen and Slade, but Doug and I have gone on double dates with them once we stopped filming and consider them true friends!

Let's not put our Maker in a box and hold Him to our pathetic little guidelines. Let's open our minds and be looking for which path He desires us to walk and gladly take bold steps in faith wherever He leads us to go.

Discussion Guide

- Share a time in your life when you felt torn about making a decision. How did you know what to do? How did your relationship with God change?

- James 1:5 promises us, "If any of you lacks wisdom, you should ask God, who gives generously to all without finding fault, and it will be given to you." When you need wisdom in your life, where do you typically go? Have you ever prayed to God about something and felt He answered?

- Isaiah 64:8 says, "Yet you, LORD, are our Father. We are the clay, you are the potter; we are all the work of your hand." How in your life have you demonstrated God's work?

- Lydia describes making sacrifices because of faith. Read Matthew 16:24–26, where Jesus says, "If anyone would come after me, let him deny himself and take up his cross and follow me. For whoever would save his life will lose it, but whoever loses his life for my sake will find it. For what will it profit a man if he gains the whole world and forfeits his soul? Or what shall a man give in return for his soul?" (ESV).

What have you given up because of your walk for Jesus?

- Psalm 40:8 says, "I delight to do your will, O my God; your law is within my heart" (ESV). Do you sense God's will in your heart? Are there times when you'd rather do not God's will but your own instead? How do you get through these moments?

six

Burning Bush Moment

Courage comes from a heart that is convinced it is loved.
—*Beth Moore*

ONCE DOUG AND I decided to pass on filming season 9 of *The Real Housewives of Orange County*, through the sadness came a peace in our household. We had grown accustomed to rushing out the door, juggling busy schedules, and just making it all work somehow. Doug and I had gotten used to the constant shuffle of pick-ups, drop-offs, babysitters, and events. But when we passed on the show, life went right back to the way things had been before. I had drastically changed, and Doug and I had gone through this crazy rabbit hole of reality TV, but our life was pretty much the same as it used to be before the show. Of course, life with two kids under four is hectic, but when the *Housewives* train departed from the station of our home, I suddenly found myself having nowhere to rush off to and more free time on my hands.

There was one afternoon during these first weeks of transition that I will always treasure. It was about a week after the media announced we were quitting the show. My younger son, Maverick, went down for his nap, and my oldest son, Stirling, was still at school. Our home was quiet, which was unusual for me, particularly coming out of that past year of rushing around at such a frantic pace. I had already had some quiet time with the Lord in the morning, but since I had this unexpected break with nothing to do and no distractions, I lay down on the floor and cried out to God.

I don't typically lie facedown on my bedroom rug, but that afternoon, I felt the posture was appropriate. I had nothing left in my spirit to give regarding worship, yet I still felt reverence toward my Maker. I was filled with all sorts of questions and doubts, yet I knew He was still with me on this path. Jesus had shown up so many times before in my life. I didn't want to be disrespectful or doubtful, but I was upset with God. I still didn't understand it. So I poured out my heart to Him.

"Why? Why put me through all this? What is Your plan? Where are You in all this? You don't make any sense, Lord! You called me out here, and now I feel abandoned. You have led me to the desert and then left me here alone. I know You called me out of the palace, but for what? What is the point of all this? I would rather be in the palace than here in the desert."

It was a very honest and emotional prayer, full of doubt and anger. I took all that emotion to God, because I had nowhere else to go. I lay there in my bedroom and connected to my King in a real and honest way.

Afterward I felt nothing profound, mostly just a good cry. God didn't visibly appear to me or speak directly to my heart. He just remained quiet and listened to me vent, I assumed.

When I finished praying, I got up and decided to call one of my best friends, Amber. She encouraged me and gave me some verses and made me feel better, as girlfriends do. She had walked with me through the whole *Housewives* journey and knew what I was going through. We talked for maybe thirty minutes, but one of the verses she said stood out to me: "There has never been the slightest doubt in my mind that the God who started this great work in you would keep at it and bring it to a flourishing finish on the very day Christ Jesus appears" (Philippians 1:6 MSG).

Amber reminded me that my journey wasn't over. God had started something in me the day I started following Him, and He wasn't done with me yet. Just because my situation and emotions were telling me one thing didn't mean that God's promises, presence, or plan had changed. He was still a good God. He was still a loving God. He was still with me, and I was still part of His plan. God's character wasn't based on my own situations or emotions. He hadn't led me out to the desert for nothing. He had started something, and He would see that through. That is who He is, and He never changes.

I hung up with Amber. Somehow our conversation had led me to know deep down inside that now was the time: "I'm going to write my book!" I declared. Amber and I hadn't even talked about that, but that was what I felt stirring in my heart.

My Burning Bush Moment

I've always wanted to write a book. Ever since I became a Christian at age fifteen, I carried a notebook with me everywhere and would jot down notes from sermons or quotes from people I had heard. I have boxes and boxes filled with notebooks with pages covered in prayers and notes, journaling and verses going back twenty years.

Doug has always wondered why I insist on keeping all these notebooks, but that afternoon it dawned on me. I had been researching and preparing to write a book for as long as I've been walking with Jesus, and now He had given me the platform to do it and be heard!

Suddenly I had a surge of energy and purpose. I rushed to our garage, pulled out one of the boxes filled with my old notebooks, and I grabbed out a handful. I carried as many as I could into our kitchen, stood at our kitchen island, and started flipping through the journal on the top of the pile.

The journal I started reading was from more than six years ago, before I even had kids. In it, I found an outline of what would become this book. I knew I would one day write a book, so I had jotted down an outline I had felt stirring within my soul at the time. It was just a dream and something I put onto paper. I then turned the page from my journal and read a quote that I had circled and put stars around.

I read in my own handwriting: "You can't have a burning bush moment in the *palace*. You must be in the desert."

God had led me to the desert and given me a burning bush moment! I was able to ask Him questions and experience a closeness with Him that could only happen on the ground, crying, in my own personal desert. He had led me out of the palace and comfort of my life and brought me to need Him desperately. He brought me to a place where I yearned for Him so much, I was facedown crying out to Him with all my soul in my bedroom on a random Tuesday afternoon. I can confidently tell you that I would not have been doing that unless I needed Him.

God's Outlandish Call

Have you even been in a desperate place, out of explanations and hope? When you have tried everything, so the only thing left could be a divine act of a holy God?

I believe there are aspects of God that you can't understand when everything is going great. You really need specific circumstances to experience certain qualities in your Maker. For example, how can you deeply understand God is a provider if you aren't desperate for

Him to provide for you in your life in some way? How can God show you a burning bush unless you are in the desert? That just doesn't happen in the palace.

The story of Moses and the burning bush is found in Exodus 3. I encourage you to read the whole story, if you have not yet, but I want to focus on the middle part of the chapter. Moses is tending his sheep in the desert, and God appears to him in a bush that is on fire but not consumed by the fire. Moses encounters the Great I AM, and his life is forever altered.

Exodus 3:7–12 says:

Then the LORD told him, "I have certainly seen the oppression of my people in Egypt. I have heard their cries of distress because of their harsh slave drivers. Yes, I am aware of their suffering. So I have come down to rescue them from the power of the Egyptians and lead them out of Egypt into their own fertile and spacious land. It is a land flowing with milk and honey— the land where the Canaanites, Hittites, Amorites, Perizzites, Hivites, and Jebusites now live. Look! The cry of the people of Israel has reached me, and I have seen how harshly the

Egyptians abuse them. Now go, for I am sending you to Pharaoh. You must lead my people Israel out of Egypt."

But Moses protested to God, "Who am I to appear before Pharaoh? Who am I to lead the people of Israel out of Egypt?"

God answered, "I will be with you. And this is your sign that I am the one who has sent you: When you have brought the people out of Egypt, you will worship God at this very mountain." (NLT)

God met Moses in the desert, where He heard Moses' cry and the cry of His people. The Lord told Moses that He wanted him to lead His people out of slavery. God's call for Moses was similar to His call for Nehemiah to rebuild the city walls.

God's Call for You

You have a similar calling, friends. I am not sure what it looks like for you personally, what your gifts are, or how the Lord wants to use you, but I can guarantee you that God wants to use you. He has a plan for you and desires to take you on a great adventure with Him. He loves you and knows you. You and I must be courageous and rooted and established in His love to live boldly for Christ!

Pursuing God's call in our lives is never easy. Like Moses, we need to face our fears and step up to God's will for our lives. I love the part of this story where Moses protests to God and says, "Who am I?" (Exodus 3:11). I think many times that is what we say about God's call in our lives. We have these big dreams and hopes and desires, but we don't think we can accomplish them.

Bible scholars believe that Moses had a stutter. Really picture this for a moment. Moses has made a new life for himself in the desert. He is a murderer and an outlaw in his old land. God appears to him and tells Moses that he not only is to go back to the land he has been running from and appear before the king—but he is to declare to the king, through his stutter, that all the slaves are to be set free.

How crazy, outlandish, and unreal does that calling sound? Sometimes God calls us to do something that doesn't make sense, but He gives us the same promise and hope that He gave Moses. In Exodus 3:12, "God answered, 'I will be with you.'" There are many other promises that build on this hope. Romans 8:31 says, "If God is for us, who can be against us?"

We know that God has called us. We know that He will be with us, and once He starts something in us He will see it through to completion (Philippians 1:6). We know that if God is for us, then what else could matter? Because of his weakness Moses had to utterly depend on God, so there was no doubt in Moses' mind that this call was from the Lord. Sometimes we need that! We need to be in a situation where all we have is God. And then He acts and we know it was because of Him that we were able to act or pray or love or forgive.

Trusting God

That is the place where this book comes from, my friends: the place in my spiritual desert where God brought me and I was poured out before Him. He led me here, to you. I have prayed for every person who will read this book and my story. We all have stories and it is through sharing our experiences that we can show each other aspects of God. What a gift that is!

Our God is big. He is vast and we can't even begin to understand Him. The Lord puts it this way to Job in chapter 38:

Where were you when I laid the earth's foundation? Tell me, if you understand. Who marked off its dimensions? Surely you know! Who stretched a measuring line across it? On what were its footings set, or who laid its cornerstone—while the morning stars sang together and all the angels shouted for joy? Who shut up the sea behind doors when it burst forth from the womb, when I made the clouds its garment and wrapped it in thick darkness, when I fixed limits for it and set its doors and bars in place, when I said, "This far you may come and no farther; here is where your proud waves halt"? (vv. 4–11)

God is God—and we are not. We must know Him and trust Him. Many times He will give us just enough to take one step.

God doesn't always reveal the whole story to us or mark out the entire journey for us to see. That wouldn't require faith or relationship. Yet God always shows us that He is trustworthy enough for us to follow on the journey with Him, one step at a time.

Discussion Guide

- Philippians 1:6 says, "There has never been the slightest doubt in my mind that the God who started this great work in you would keep at it and bring it to a flourishing finish on the very day Christ Jesus appears" (MSG). How does this verse encourage you? Do the actions in your life show that you truly believe it?

- Lydia talks a lot about being led out to the "desert." When was a season in your life where you spent time in the desert? Did that season lead to a burning bush moment for you in any way?

- Lydia writes, "How can you deeply understand God is a provider if you aren't desperate for Him to provide for you in your life?" In what ways are you desperate for God to provide in your life? How have you seen Him provide?

- Taking and pursuing God's call in our life is never easy. Like Moses, we need to face our fears and step up to God's will for our lives. What are some fears you have that are hindering you from walking boldly in the will of God?

- In Exodus 3:12, God declares, "I will be with you." When was a time you felt God was with you? If you have never experienced this, why do you suppose that is?
- What is one way that you can step out boldly in faith this week?

seven

Our Identity

Anything done for another is done
for oneself.
—*Pope John Paul II*

I WENT TO THE University of San Diego. My freshman year I rushed the sorority Alpha Phi. I think like many eighteen-year-olds, I was figuring out who I was and what I stood for. I became a Christian my freshman year of high school and, at the time, was surrounded by a community that was constantly encouraging me and lifting me up. In college, I didn't have that group for support and accountability and was forced to stand up for my faith alone.

During rush I really lost myself in a lot of ways. I partied and made some unwise decisions. I wasn't standing for anything; I was falling for everything fast. During that time, my identity had nothing to do with Christ and everything to do with a typical college girl stereotype. I didn't like who I was and felt alone, shameful, and empty.

Halfway through my first semester, I went on a retreat and spent time alone with the Lord. I realized I was angry with Him for so many things and was in a season of rebellion. That weekend He called me back to His love and I was changed. I was reminded of my identity: I belonged to God.

With my newfound confidence, I came home from the retreat with a renewed vision of why God had placed me at my specific college and in my specific sorority. I was determined to be a light for Jesus in that place.

That Monday back from my weekend retreat, we had our chapter meeting. God had placed in my heart the desire to start a Bible study with my sorority sisters, and He wasn't giving me even a day to get cold feet. I would guess most of these girls had no idea I was even a Christian, and here I was, a lowly freshman, called to stand up in front of about one hundred of my sorority sisters and announce I was starting a Bible study!

Our sorority president asked if there was any new business, and I nervously raised my hand. I stood up and said that I was starting a Bible study—and if anyone was interested in joining, they could come talk to me after our meeting. Through my college years, there was a group of about five of us who met weekly. We prayed for each other, studied the Word together, and developed deep friendships.

I realized my identity had shifted somewhere during my first semester in college, from being rooted in Jesus to being some college sorority girl. I had wanted to be part of the "cool crowd." I had cared what everyone thought of me, and I had wanted to fit in and have this epic college experience. But I was lost and drowning until I came back to my Maker.

Finding Our Identity

Living in a culture where we are able to constantly measure our worth or our popularity, it is hard to really focus on what God says about us. What is truth? What is real character? If I placed my value or identity on how many likes my Facebook or Instagram photo receives, I would be stressed to get an epic shot where it looks like my family is perfect and we are having an amazing time. I would compare my "likes" to other friends' "likes" and have a competition inside about who has more value. I would read the comments on my posts and sometimes be built up and other times torn down by the nastiness that happens through the anonymity of the Internet. I know a girl who is secure in who Jesus has made her to be, and she is breathtakingly beautiful. I just want to be around her. Yet you can't capture that type of graceful godliness on an Instagram post.

How do we find our identity? Stop and think about that. What do you place your worth and confidence in? Do you determine your value by the number of Instagram followers you have, or is your value based on something greater? In your own mind, what defines who you are?

As women, it's so easy to slip into finding our value in physical appearances. If I have a new outfit on and am feeling particularly beautiful today, I have an extra pep in my step. And then I spill my coffee on it. Is that going to ruin my day?

Or what if my children are being perfect angels and making me seem like the perfect mom? Does that give me a sense of worth? Good one. Have you ever tried to make a two-year-old boy an angel?

Having an ideal job.

A great marriage.

A stunning body.

Designer clothes.

There are so many things we can pursue. And many of these things are good. I want to be a good mom to my boys. I love expressing my moods through fashion. I don't think there is anything wrong with those things. However, they become an issue when we allow those things to define our worth.

The Bible shows us four ways we can begin to find our identity in Christ: being a servant, fearing the Lord, praying regularly, and having childlike faith.

Being a Servant

Jesus says in Luke 12:34, "For where your treasure is, there your heart will be also." I believe Jesus is saying that *it matters what matters to us.* What do you value? Do you value being a leader and being looked up to by others? Or do you value being a humble servant to others, without the need for recognition or applause or fame?

We can learn so much through Christ's example. He was a servant. His whole life, not just His death, was built on serving. He had a servant's heart.

Are we living out a servant-hearted attitude in our daily lives? Mark 10:43–45 says, "Whoever wants to become great among you must be your servant, and whoever wants to be first must be slave of all. For even the Son of Man did not come to be served, but to serve, and to give his life as a ransom for many." If Christ became human and dedicated His whole existence to a life of service, who do I think I am not to serve?

Fearing the Lord

Sometimes we need to step back and examine our lives, and that will show us what we truly believe deep down. If I really believe that God's Word is true and that Jesus is King of kings, then my day-to-day life would change drastically. I would have a fear of the Lord. I would realize how big and powerful and holy and vast He is, and I would fall to my knees and worry about things of eternal kingdom purpose. My to-do list that I run over and over in my head on a daily basis would seem so trite compared to what God desires of me. I need to have a fear of the Lord.

Do we contemplate how holy God is? Are we cultivating reverence toward Him in our daily lives? Proverbs 9:10 tells us, "The fear of the LORD is the beginning of wisdom." I want to be wise. If I have a space within my soul to be reverent toward God, that is the beginning of wisdom. If we truly are contemplating how holy and big and loving the character of God is, we not only would fear Him but we would want to know Him.

Praying Regularly

Each of us must ask ourselves, *Do I have a regular prayer time? Do I just send up prayers at random, or do I set aside a consistent time to pray as a priority in my daily routine?* Mark 1:35 says, "Very early in the morning, while it was still dark, Jesus got up, left the house and went off to a solitary place, where he prayed." Jesus prayed often. He would retreat after talks to pray. He would spend all day teaching and healing people and then wake up early and pray. He yearned to be connected to His Father and so must we!

If Jesus, who is the Son of God, would wake up while it was still dark out so He could have His quiet times with the Lord, why am I not setting my alarm to get up and pray? How am I going to reflect the Father if I am not in union with Him, spending time with Him? We make lunch dates with our girlfriends; let's make a prayer date with our Creator. And what an honor it is that He would take the time to spend with us!

Having Childlike Faith

Matthew 18:2–4 describes Jesus' desire that we have a humble, childlike heart: "And calling to him a child, he put him in the midst of them and said, 'Truly, I say to you, unless you turn and become like children, you will never enter the kingdom of heaven. Whoever humbles himself like this child is the greatest in the kingdom of heaven'" (ESV).

Being a servant. Fearing the Lord. Prayer. Childlike faith. Are you cultivating these things in your life? Would your friends use these words to describe you?

Becoming Like Jesus

Have you ever hung out with someone so much you start acting like that person? I often get teased that I say the word *like* a lot. I decided to try to work on it, so I became aware that I do use it often. I also started to notice that all my friends say it a lot as well. We hang out with one another so much we have adopted the same speech and mannerisms. You tend to pick up traits and sayings from those you spend the most time with.

Matthew 6:19–20 says, "Do not lay up for yourselves treasures on earth, where moth and rust destroy and where thieves break in and steal, but lay up for yourselves treasures in heaven, where neither moth nor rust destroys and where thieves do not break in and steal" (ESV). What could have more eternal significance than spending time with Jesus? This is crucial for our faith journey.

I know I spend way more time in the morning worrying about my makeup than I do about orphans. I think more about my arms being toned than I think about how I can help the elderly. I go to the gym three times a week, yet how many times do I volunteer a week? And this isn't to put a guilt trip on you or me. It is simply trying to peel back the layers of who we say we are and what we say we believe so we can live it out.

Jesus calls the Pharisees' faith vain, empty, and hollow. In Matthew 15:8–9, He says, "These people honor me with their lips, but their hearts are far from me. They worship me in vain." Many of us are modern-day Pharisees! We are like the people who went to church yet didn't live out their faith in practical ways.

What would Jesus say about your faith?

Jesus knows our hearts. Again, this is another churchy thing to say, but there is a lot of truth to these churchy sayings. God knows our hearts. We can't fool God.

Proverbs 20:27 says, "The human spirit is the lamp of the LORD that sheds light on one's inmost being." The New Living Translation puts it like this: "The LORD's light penetrates the human spirit, exposing every hidden motive." God knows our hearts and He wants us to pour them out to Him, even our complaints. He knows them anyway, and He delights in our childlike faith in Him. Our trust. Our relationship. We keep wanting to make God like us. We base our love or acceptance of people on how they act. We can't humanize God. He is Lord of all and is better at loving than we are. He will still love you if you complain to Him.

Psalm 142:1–3 says, "I cry aloud to the LORD; I lift my voice to the LORD for mercy. I pour out before him my complaint; before him I tell my trouble. When my spirit grows faint within me, it is you who watch over my way."

The Bible is a story of God wanting to have a relationship with us. He can handle us telling Him our troubles. All of them—big and small. Have you ever met a child who will just tell you like it is? No filter—just honest, raw truth. That is what God desires from us.

Asking God to Change My Heart

When I was asked back to do season 9 of *The Real Housewives of Orange County*, I wanted to do it. Being on the show was everything the world tells us to desire, and it was everything my heart desired.

The show was fame. People everywhere wanted a picture with me. I felt validated and important.

The show was glamour. I loved getting to dress up and go to fabulous events.

The show was fun for me, and I wanted to do it. But deep, deep down—so quiet I could almost silence it—I knew in my heart it wasn't God's plan for me to go back. I knew that God was calling me to walk away from the show. But I didn't want to!

Being on the show was everything I've ever wanted. How could God ask me to walk away from all that?

The truth is, we can't fool God and we can't outrun God. So I began to pray and ask God to change my heart. If He didn't desire me to go back, then I wanted my heart to have the peace and strength to walk away. I often prayed using the words of the dad who asks

Jesus in Mark 9:24: "I do believe; help me overcome my unbelief!"

I was able to take a situation that could have left me bitter and angry with God and turn it into a time of prayer. I experienced a time of realness and honesty with my Maker. Instead of being angry or bitter, I asked God to help me overcome my unbelief.

The night before Jesus faced His crucifixion, He spent time in prayer. He knew what the next day would bring Him and prayed, "Father, if you are willing, take this cup from me; yet not my will, but yours be done" (Luke 22:42). Jesus asked God to change the plan, but in the same breath He submitted to and placed His trust in God.

During my journey of Housewife decisions, I clung to Philippians 1:6: "being confident of this, that he who began a good work in you will carry it on to completion until the day of Christ Jesus." I asked God to change my heart, and then I claimed His promises over my life and experienced a sweet and tender time with Jesus.

Born to Be the Difference

We were born to make a difference—to *be* the difference. Jesus proclaimed that He would send His Spirit to guide us and lead us to do big, powerful things. Does your life reflect that? Believe in His Spirit inside you, friend. What a gift!

Here are a few verses that help us understand the Holy Spirit's role in our lives:

- When he, the Spirit of truth, comes, he will guide you into all the truth. (John 16:13)
- When you believed, you were marked in him with a seal, the promised Holy Spirit, who is a deposit guaranteeing our inheritance until the redemption of those who are God's possession—to the praise of his glory. (Ephesians 1:13–14)
- Those who live according to the flesh have their minds set on what the flesh desires; but those who live in accordance with the Spirit have their minds set on what the Spirit desires. The mind governed by the flesh is death, but the mind governed by the Spirit is life and peace. (Romans 8:5–6)
- I am filled with power, with the Spirit of the LORD, and with justice and might. (Micah 3:8)

The Holy Spirit is real, and if you are a Christian, He lives in you. If you have accepted Jesus Christ as your

Lord and Savior, you have the seal of the Holy Spirit on you (Ephesians 1:13). This is the truth we hold on to. The father of lies is trying to convince us that the voice we are hearing isn't from God. But the feeling deep down that guides us to do God's will—that is the Holy Spirit inside of us telling us to serve, to talk to the person, to step out and do the hard thing. That is God stirring in our souls. He tells us He is going to guide us.

Listen and Act!

Sometimes, when we hear God's voice in our hearts, we question it. John 12:29 says, "When the crowd heard the voice, some thought it was thunder, while others declared an angel had spoken to him" (NLT).

We are hearing Him! Be bold and courageous! Don't try to justify or explain away the voice of God stirring in your heart. Listen and act!

First John 5:14–15 says, "This is the confidence we have in approaching God: that if we ask anything according to his will, he hears us. And if we know that he hears us—whatever we ask—we know that we have what we asked of him."

God is actively pursuing us. We get to approach Him and He hears us! Can we even begin to comprehend the goodness of that Scripture passage? Imagine you are standing before the ocean as the sky starts turning into a magical painting around sunset hour, using a palette of purples and pinks. You hear and see the vast ocean and the waves crashing onto the sand, and all creation is screaming glory to its Maker. You witness and feel and see all this grandness—and then you step back and connect the fact that the God who created all this is the same God who created you, knows you, and loves you.

The world is so magnificent and yet so full of despair at times. God allows us to have a choice. We can serve Him and give our lives to the things He cares about—or we can go on with the rat race and pursue our culture's list of temporary occupations. God leaves the option to us.

We make a decision every day. Every moment. What we choose to think about, worry about, and pursue is our choice. We are actively living out what we believe. Those choices will determine who we are, who we serve, and where our identity lies.

Discussion Guide

- Who is someone you look up to because his or her identity is in Christ? What is a tangible way you have seen that in this person's life?

- What are some things people can put their identity in? How can we become a community where we place our identity in Jesus and encourage one another as women of faith in that?

- Lydia gave a lot of Scripture verses in the chapter. Share one verse that struck a chord with you. Why did it?

- Having a fear of the Lord is discussed a lot in the Old Testament but is not discussed much in today's Christian culture. Do you have a fear of the Lord? What is the difference of being scared of God and having a healthy, reverent fear of Him?

- Have you ever felt guided by the Holy Spirit in your life? What is something bold you have done because you felt God stirring within you?

eight

Love, Love, Love

The greatest of these is love.
—*The apostle Paul*

DOUG AND I met while volunteering for Young Life—an organization that introduces kids to Jesus and helps them grow in their faith. I was twenty-one and had just graduated from the University of San Diego and moved to Orange County. I was new to the area and hadn't met a lot of people in Newport Beach yet. I walked into the leadership meeting, and I remember the scene as if it happened moments ago. A lot of people were buzzing about the room, and in the back there were five guys sitting on a couch. It was like the crowd parted in the room when I walked in, and I saw Doug. I didn't see anyone else, I just saw him and in my heart I prayed, *Thank You, God.* I knew that he was mine and made for me.

But it wasn't "love at first sight" at all for Doug. I like to think it's because I'm so in tune with Jesus that I knew (ha!), but Doug took things a little more slowly. We would see each other every week at the Young Life club meetings, and I would always be nervous and try to calm myself down because I knew Wednesday night I would be seeing him. I would walk over and say hello, and he would say, "Hey, Linda." Listen to my heart tearing in two. He didn't even know my name! I was giving thanksgiving praise to the Lord that I had found my future husband, and he didn't even know my name!

Through the years Doug has really shown me what true love is like, what it means to be in a godly relationship, and how to communicate well when angry. He has shown me how to experience conflict in a way that is productive and not just emotional. I tend to be a bit dramatic at times, and he maintains his cool and has led me wisely through his example.

Showing Jesus' Love to the World

Jesus is known for His love, but Christians are not. That is sad. The term *Christians*, some believe to mean "little Christs." We are Jesus Christ's representatives making His appeal to the world. The Bible tells us, "By this everyone will know that you are my disciples, if you love one another" (John 13:35).

How do I share love with the world? Do people I come into contact with throughout my day know Jesus, living in me, because of my love toward them? Do I act differently now than I did before because of my relationship with God? Am I being mindful of the fact that I represent Christ to those around me? Or am I in such a hurry to drop my boys at school and get through my list of errands before work that loving someone, and stopping to listen to him or her, is the last thing on my agenda? I have to be mindful. I have to wake up every morning and set my priorities.

Below are some of the verses I read regularly to help me remember that I am a "little Christ" to those around me:

- I have been crucified with Christ. It is no longer I who live, but Christ who lives in me. And the life

I now live in the flesh I live by faith in the Son of God, who loved me and gave himself for me. (Galatians 2:20 ESV)

- See what kind of love the Father has given to us, that we should be called children of God; and so we are. The reason why the world does not know us is that it did not know him. (1 John 3:1 ESV)

- With all humility and gentleness, with patience, [bear] with one another in love. (Ephesians 4:2 ESV)

Another Scripture passage about love is the famous passage often quoted during wedding ceremonies: "Love is patient, love is kind. It does not envy, it does not boast, it is not proud. It does not dishonor others, it is not self-seeking, it is not easily angered, it keeps no record of wrongs. Love does not delight in evil but rejoices with the truth. It always protects, always trusts, always hopes, always perseveres" (1 Corinthians 13:4–7).

This passage is often read at weddings because these aspects of love are so vital to a marriage relationship. We get to experience real love through marriage. If we desire to maintain a healthy, loving marriage, we have to demonstrate the love that is described in 1 Corinthians

13. Our culture's worldview on love has been watered down and jaded. It is good, especially at the beginning of a marriage, to define what it means to love someone and to commit to love that person for the rest of our lives under that definition.

The Five A's

When Doug and I were engaged, we went to premarital counseling. One of the most helpful tools we learned through counseling was the concept of the five A's. We learned that when a conflict was starting to arise we could do the five A's with each other and this would help us communicate. We were also encouraged to do the five A's every so often, just to clear the air. We found this very helpful in our marriage. If you aren't married yet, put this in your pocket and try it out when the time comes and you need it. I think it has come in handy for us in our marriage.

If you both agree to do the five A's, you will constantly be getting things off your chest and communicating effectively. Many times I will not talk about things with Doug but add them to my laundry list of annoyances in my mind. Then Doug won't take the trash out one morning and I'll explode on him. In his mind he is thinking, *I just didn't take out the trash; why is she so upset?* In my mind, that was just the match that set me off. The real issue was something that happened two days ago but I never talked about it; I was just holding it inside allowing to fester within me. The five A's don't allow that to happen. You will be communicating constantly. You may feel kind of silly going through these but I feel this strategy has allowed Doug and me to deal with many small issues before they became big issues.

Here are the five A's.

Affirm

Before you poke someone with a needle it is best to give him or her a little numbing cream! This is the thought behind the first step, affirmation. First, we are to tell our spouse something we love about him—a quality of who he is that we admire.

Ask

Next, you ask each other, "How have I hurt you in the past seven days?" This allows both of you to describe a time when you felt slighted or hurt. Sometimes it is a big thing or a deep issue, and other times it is something tiny. You each take a turn to talk while the other listens.

This is key. This isn't a conversation or an argument. You each just get to share your feelings.

Apologize

After you each have heard how you have hurt your beloved, then you both apologize and ask for forgiveness.

Affection

You then show each other affection. This is very important. After a disagreement, many times the last thing I want to do is hug my husband. But it is important for us to show affection to each other, especially after being so open and vulnerable.

Amen

You both then pray together. Ask God to come into, guard, and protect your marriage.

Vulnerable Love

There are many relationships outside of marriage where we have the opportunity to love. We can also experience love through family, and by becoming a mother. We can show love to a friend, as we open our hearts to one another. Love is all around us.

C. S. Lewis writes in *The Four Loves*, "To love at all is to be vulnerable. Love anything and your heart will be wrung and possibly be broken. If you want to make sure of keeping it intact, you must give your heart to no one, not even to an animal. Wrap it carefully round with hobbies and little luxuries; avoid all entanglements; lock it up safe in the casket or coffin of your selfishness. But in that casket—safe, dark, motionless, airless—it will change. It will not be broken; it will become unbreakable, impenetrable, irredeemable."[1] To love is to be vulnerable.

Vulnerable love is fully giving yourself to someone and allowing that person to see all your insecurities and imperfections and you see theirs, yet you still choose love. Through sickness and health. Good times and bad.

The Bible uses the term *unfailing love* thirty-two times—but it is never attributed to humans, only to God. God has the love thing down, while we have a lot to learn in the love department!

Three Kinds of Love

To better understand the term *love*, we need to break it down. The English language has one word, *love*, to describe many different emotions. For example, I love

101

gooey, warm brownies, but I also love my husband. These are two very different feelings, but in English they are described with the same word. The Greek language uses completely different terms to describe the various kinds of love.

Let's break down three kinds of love.

Eros Love

Eros love is where we get the word *erotic*. Eros is the bow-chicka-wow-wow kind of love. In Greek mythology, Eros was the god of love, and in Greek the word means "longing and desire." God created this eros love inside of us.

Hold on, I'd like to add a disclaimer. In 1 Corinthians 7:8–9, the apostle Paul notes that it is wise for people to marry to fulfill their God-given desire for this type of love.

Eros love is a necessary part of a godly marriage. For those of us who are married, we need to pray that we would feel this desire and longing for our husband, to get butterflies at his touch. Obviously, our relationship will go through stages, ebbs and flows. We need to be on guard and in prayer. This is part of our being, the way we are created. Yet it is to be unleashed only in the context of marriage. Only under a commitment like that is it safe. When we act on this love, it is physical and yet spiritual. We become entangled with our mate, and if we merely follow our fleshly desires and seek this love without the commitment of marriage, we will be torn apart.

Once you get married, that doesn't mean you then have conquered this eros love. You and your spouse have to work at your marriage and your longing desire for each other. I remember having my first son and then going to my ob-gyn for the six-week checkup. The last thing I was thinking about was having eros love with my husband, if you get my drift. My breasts were engorged with milk, and I was crying for no reason due to all the hormones. I was a new mom with a new body, and I wasn't feeling any "longing desire" for my husband. My doctor gave me the green light to go for it with my man. I looked at her with apprehension. I wasn't ready yet! She told me that it was important for me and for my husband to bond in that physical way. This was true. It is important, in the context of marriage, to give yourself physically to each other. It is a spiritual part of our being. My doctor told me, "It's not just for you but for your husband. You are first and foremost his bride, and then you're a mother."

Philia Love

Philia love is friendship or affection. You can be a friend of a person or a thing. For example, I am a friend of warm, gooey brownies. I also am a friend of the girls in my moms' group. We share a love for the Word and one another. When they are happy and experience joy, so do I. When they are hurting, I am filled with sorrow. Their pain is my pain. I love them. They are my family and my sisters. This is a philia love.

I pray that as a woman you have found a community of friends you can go through life with. That makes the sweet moments that much more tender, and the hard times that much more bearable. The philia love of affection and friendship is an important part of who we are.

Agape Love

Agape love is found in perhaps the most famous scripture of the New Testament: "For God so loved [*agape*] the world that he gave his one and only Son, that whoever believes in him shall not perish but have eternal life" (John 3:16).

Agape love is how God loves. His love for us is perfect. Not self-seeking. True, pure, noble, and best. And

Scripture tells us that God's agape love provokes a response. Because God loved the world, He was called to action on behalf of those He loved. Similarly, when we have agape love for others, we are called to action on behalf of those we love. We can't say we believe in Christ on Sundays and then focus only on ourselves the other six days of the week.

If your life is going to make sense to unbelievers, then you should show concern for others. When Christ comes into our lives, He turns them upside down. He says the first will be last, and the last will be first (Matthew 19:30; 20:16). He uses Himself as an example of how to serve. We must be "little Christs" and we do that through our love that results in a response.

Acting Out Your Love

Oswald Chambers wrote, "No love of the natural heart is safe unless the human heart has been satisfied by God first."[2] We cannot go around acting out this agape love if we haven't experienced it through Christ first. We need to love out of the overflow of our hearts. We need to be filled up first and then through that, an outpouring of our love to others will be natural and organic. God doesn't call us to give what we do not have. He fills us up with His Spirit of love, and out of that abundance we can't help but love God and others.

Take an account of your life. Are you acting out agape love toward people in your life? Is your life dramatically different because of Christ? What do you think about? What do you worry about? What do you do when you worry? How do you talk? What words do you use? Everything is important. Everything matters. God wants everything in our lives to be rooted in love.

The greatest thing you'll ever learn is to love and be loved in return.

Discussion Guide

- Who is someone in your life whom you know loves you unconditionally?

- Lydia described the five A's she and Doug do in their marriage. How do you communicate with the people you love in your life? Do you hold things in when conflict arises? Do you lash out in anger? Do you have good role models in your life who are communicating their feelings to you in healthy ways?

- If you are married, how do you keep the eros love alive for your spouse? Do you make sure you are going on regular date nights together? Are you both making the "longing desire" a priority within your marriage?

- As women, our lifeline is to have friends we walk through life with. Describe a time you saw your philia love for a friend play out in a tangible way in your life.

- We see through Christ's example that agape love provokes a response. How have you responded to God's unconditional love in your life? Share specific examples when your actions have been affected by this love.

- Write 1 Corinthians 13:4–6: "*Love* is patient, *love* is kind. It does not envy, it does not boast, it is not proud. It does not dishonor others, it is not self-seeking, it is not easily angered, it keeps no record of wrongs. *Love* does not delight in evil but rejoices with the truth." Now insert your name every time you see the word *love*. Try to live that out this week.

nine

Family Matters

*I used to want to fix people, but
now I just want to be with them.*
—Bob Goff

I DIDN'T GROW UP in a typical Christian home. My mom is an Italian Catholic, so our family would go to Mass occasionally. Spirituality was often discussed in my home, and we would always pray before meals and bedtime. My family believes in God; they just do things a little differently in many areas, including religion.

I started going to Young Life camps in high school and gave my life to Jesus when I was fifteen years old. I really looked up to my Young Life leader, who was a UCLA student named Casey. Whenever Casey came home from Los Angeles, she would drive to my house and take me to church.

When I was in high school, Miles McPherson would speak weekly at a night service at a church called Horizon. Miles is a charismatic man who used to play professional football for the San Diego Chargers. He is funny and fun, and his talks would have us laughing out loud and taking notes at the same time. He spoke right into my heart many times, and God used his way with words to stir my love for Jesus.

The first time I went with Casey to hear Miles speak was around Christmas in 1996. She was home for Christmas break, so she picked me up at my house. We walked into the service and sat in the back of the gymnasium on the bleachers. Miles was teaching from the first chapter of the gospel of Matthew, which can be quite boring for a Christmas service. Matthew 1 gives the genealogy of Jesus. For example, Matthew 1:7–8 reads, "Solomon the father of Rehoboam, Rehoboam the father of Abijah, Abijah the father of Asa, Asa the father of Jehoshaphat ..."

This person is the father of this person who is the father of this person. Simple. However, I will always remember what Miles said about this passage: "You know why I believe this is in the Bible for us? So we can know that Jesus' family is *messed up*! Just like ours! This guy was a murderer. And this dude was a liar . . ." And on and on it went. He picked a few of the people listed in Jesus' genealogy and described their stories.

Jesus' family had issues. Just like yours. Just like mine. I was laughing during that church service, and my heart was also somehow lighter. I didn't have to come from a perfect Christian family to have a God who understands, loves, and wants to use me for His purpose. Whatever family you were born into, God planned it that way. He chose you to learn from your experiences with your family. You are to be a light to your parents, siblings, and extended family, as they are to be a light to you.

A Personal God

We don't have a God who can't relate to us. We don't have a God who sees our issues and turns away, asking us to get it together before we approach His throne. Instead, we have a God who gets us. He knows us. He understands.

The Bible isn't a story of human beings seeking God but of God searching for rebellious human beings. It doesn't matter where you came from or what you have done. Hebrews 4:16 says, "Let us then with confidence draw near to the throne of grace, that we may receive mercy and find grace to help in time of need" (ESV). You and I are called to approach God's throne with confidence. How amazing is that?

Ephesians 2:8–9 says, "For it is by grace you have been saved, through faith—and this is not from yourselves, it is the gift of God—not by works, so that no one can boast." The Lord knows our hearts, yet He gives us grace. Our whole life is a response to His grace. Every moment we are making choices that reflect what we believe. Some people know about God. They know the Bible inside and out, but they don't believe God. What does your life say you believe?

Romans 8:34 says, "Who then is the one who condemns? No one. Christ Jesus who died—more than that, who was raised to life—is at the right hand of God and is also interceding for us." Jesus isn't condemning us; He is interceding on our behalf to claim us as His! If anyone has the right to call out our faults, it is our Savior, Jesus. Yet what does Scripture say He does? He is interceding for us. *Interceding* means to intervene on behalf of another. Think about this: Jesus Christ sits at the right hand of God. Try to picture in your own mind the throne of the Lord and all the worship that is encompassing Him. The Bible tells us that those in heaven praise Him, saying, "Holy, holy, holy is the Lord God Almighty" (Revelation 4:8). When we approach this amazing, beautiful, awe-inspiring throne, Jesus is interceding on our behalf. Some people describe Him as our Lawyer interceding for us before a holy Judge, but I picture it as much more personal than that. He looks into my eyes. He knows me and I know Him. He leans over and whispers into his Father's ear, *I have called Lydia, and she is Mine* (Isaiah 43:1).

Designed to Belong Together

None of us comes from a perfect family, but we are all invited into Christ's family. Community is an important part of our adventure of faith. When Jesus sent His disciples to spread the good news, He sent each of them out with a buddy. Jesus "sent them two by two" (Luke 10:1). Jesus knows that we are designed to share our lives with one another. He doesn't want us to do life alone.

It doesn't matter what political party, gender, or nationality you are. If you are a Christian, we are all united by a belief in Christ. Jesus Christ is our common denominator. We belong together as a family. If one of us is hurting, we all are; and if one of us rejoices, we all celebrate. "If one member suffers, all suffer together; if one member is honored, all rejoice together" (1 Corinthians 12:26 ESV).

We belong together. We were created to share this experience of life together with one another. You won't understand the power of community until you're part of one. Romans 12:5 says, "So we, though many, are one body in Christ, and individually members one of another" (ESV). We are a community to encourage together, cry together, and cheer one another on together. Being together makes life sweeter. We are all children of God, and that makes us all family. You belong and are needed. You have a special calling and part that only you can do.

The Importance of Community

I have had seasons in my life where I wasn't part of a community, and it is lonely. The greatest times of my life have been when I have been vulnerable enough to share my experiences with others. We are created to encourage one another and have fellowship with people beyond a Sunday service at church. We were created to share our lives with other people.

Romans 12:4–5 helps us understand the importance of community. It states, "For as in one body we have many members, and the members do not all have the same function, so we, though many, are one body in Christ, and individually members one of another" (ESV). What stands out to me about that verse is that we each have a role. If you don't live out your gifts, your choice not only affects you but the whole body of Christ misses out. It is our responsibility to function within the body of Christ.

I remember being in high school, and every Friday night after the football game everyone would head up to Pony Field. Some seniors would bring a keg and all the kids would gather around for a typical Friday night rager. At the root of that is the devil playing on our desire for community. Have you ever wondered why people go out to bars and party with strangers who become their best friends for the night? We have a God-given desire to be in fellowship with other people. The bonds that are formed over keg stands are obviously not what God intended. However, the bonds of walking through life with like-minded people are necessary for truly living.

There is something that happens to us when we are connected to a community. When we feel we are part of a bigger story, it quiets and satisfies our soul. In my own life, the people in my church are like family. Walking in the church doors on a Sunday feels like coming home. I am part of a moms' group at church that has been meeting every week for over six years. Of course there are weeks when I didn't want to go, but that connection I have with the other moms is priceless. The sacrifices I have made to be there week after week have paid me back over and over. Over time I have cultivated deep friendships, and those girls are now an extension of me. I have laughed with them and cried with them over all aspects of what life throws at us.

As I was growing up, I often heard the saying, "You may be the only Bible anyone ever reads." This prompts us to live our faith out loud, but we also receive a blessing in exposing who we are to others. I think this is another reason God is so big on communities and relationships. I was interested in getting to know Jesus because I saw Him through other people. The Christians I knew were different and I wanted to know why. If these believers in Christ hadn't shared who they were with me, then I would never have had the opportunity to find out who Jesus is.

We need to be part of a community—to belong and be known. Jen Hatmaker, in her book *Out of the Spin Cycle*, writes, "The way we love each other, serve each other, and live our lives with each other is a big deal to Jesus. At the beginning of time, creation encountered its first problem: 'It is not good for them to be alone.' Thus history began with human connection. Two are better than one, and togetherness is always superior to loneliness."[1]

Connected to the Family of Faith

When I went away to college, it was a very hard season for me. In high school I had been part of my youth group and felt a strong sense of community. Like many college freshmen, it was hard for me to find that sense of community again.

After my freshman year, I volunteered as summer staff through Young Life. For those three months I served high school kids who would come to the camp for a week at a time. The camp's summer staff was all college students who were giving up their summer to serve high schoolers in one way or another. We didn't get paid or any real recognition, but we were all there with a like-mindedness of serving Jesus through this calling. When I look back, those months on Young Life's summer staff stand out to me as a time of growth and real community. The staff quickly became a family, supporting one another and serving alongside each other. We experienced the truth of Psalm 133:1: "Behold, how good and pleasant it is when brothers [and sisters] dwell in unity!" (ESV).

Made to Be Loved

My friend was a social worker, and on her first day of the job her supervisor took her to pick up a baby who was in poor condition. My friend saw this pitiful, weak infant and couldn't believe that someone could be so cruel to abuse an innocent child. The supervisor looked at her and said, "This baby hasn't been abused. This baby has never been touched." We were made to be loved and part of a family. It is who we are created to be.

My youth pastor, Bob Schrimpf, used to say, "None of us has it all together, but together we have it all." We were created to be in relation with one another. We will spend eternity with one another praising our Lord. We yearn for relationships and real connection with one another.

Maybe you come from a very loving, safe family, or maybe you come from a messed-up family. Either way, if you are a Christian, you belong to Jesus' family!

Discussion Guide

- Describe your family growing up. Was it big? Were you close? What type of activities did you do with one another?
- Have you ever thought about belonging to God's family? Do you feel a part of it? How?
- Have there been times in your life where you felt disconnected or lonely? When? What did you do to take that feeling away?
- How has being a part of a community affected who you are?
- Lydia quotes her youth pastor saying, "None of us has it all together, but together we have it all." What does this mean to you? Do you feel this truth in your own daily life?
- This week, reach out to someone who is not in your inner circle and affirm him or her in some way.

ten

Created Beautiful

True beauty in a woman is reflected in her soul.
—Audrey Hepburn

BEFORE I BECAME a mother, I was somewhat of a "gym rat." I worked out at least five times a week, as it was my routine to go to the gym before work every morning. I had a lot of time on my hands, so I used it to tone and shape my body, and I loved being fit.

Once I got pregnant with our first son, Stirling, that routine was drastically and swiftly taken away from me.

No more boot camp Mondays; I was having a child and this was the sole purpose of my body. I traded in a burpee circuit for an ultrasound. At first I was okay with this lifestyle change, because pregnancy was beautiful and I was excited to be a mom. But about four months into the pregnancy, truthfully, I was over the whole ordeal. I missed sweating and the release that exercise brought to my day. I saw not just my belly, but my whole body getting bigger and bigger. I didn't know if I would ever look the way I did prebaby. I felt my body was being held hostage. I was moody and tired and not feeling the "pregnancy glow" so many people speak of.

Now that I have three kids, I know the beauty of a woman's body and how it changes and adjusts after pregnancy. However, I didn't have that experience to draw on my first go-around and I was honestly terrified.

After I gave birth to Stirling, my girlfriends who hadn't had children yet came over. I had shared with them my fears while pregnant and so they were complimenting my postbaby body, but in a way to ask me how I was doing with it all. I remember responding to them with a confidence I had never experienced up to that point in my life.

I had given birth and felt like superwoman. I felt stronger than I had ever felt before, because my body had housed this special, precious little soul. I felt like I understood, or got a glimpse for the first time, the true beauty of a woman's body and why God created us in such a divine and unique way. I felt truly and completely beautiful.

The Pressure to Be Beautiful

We put pressure on ourselves to be a certain size or have a certain hair color to be beautiful. As a woman, I need to overcome conditional confidence. I need to be secure in who I am and not base my self-esteem on fleeting outward appearances. I need to know in the deepest part of my soul what God has to say about my worth:

- God saw all that he had made, and it was very good. (Genesis 1:31)
- For your royal husband delights in your beauty; honor him for he is your lord. (Psalm 45:11 NLT)
- Do you not know that your bodies are temples of the Holy Spirit, who is in you, whom you have received from God? You are not your own. (1 Corinthians 6:19)
- I pray that the eyes of your heart may be enlightened, so that you will know what is the hope of His calling, what are the riches of the glory of His inheritance in the saints. (Ephesians 1:18 NASB)

- We are therefore Christ's ambassadors, as though God were making his appeal through us. (2 Corinthians 5:20)

God made us. He loves what He created in you and me. His Holy Spirit lives in us and we are His ambassadors to the world!

But my reality is that:

- Only 4 percent of women worldwide consider themselves beautiful.[1]
- The United States has the biggest cosmetic market in the world, with estimated total revenue of more than $56 billion US dollars a year.[2]
- Americans alone spent more than $12 billion on cosmetic procedures in 2013.[3]

Most of us are insecure about our physical appearance. We try to fill this void by buying makeup and having cosmetic surgery to try to live up to our culture's idea of beauty as portrayed everywhere we look. We drive down the freeway and see billboards displaying perfect airbrushed images. But the truth is, Britney Spears doesn't even look like Britney Spears in real life!

The Devil's Lies about Beauty

Ezekiel 28:12 describes the devil before his fall into sin: "You were the seal of perfection, full of wisdom and perfect in beauty." When Satan was created by God, he was an exceedingly beautiful angel. He was likely the highest of all angels, the most beautiful of all of God's creation, but he was not content in his position.

I believe that's why the devil goes after women in the area of beauty. He was the most beautiful angel, so he attacks us brutally when it comes to issues of our own beauty. He knows what it is like to be beautiful and what the quest for beauty is capable of. He knows how many chains he can wrap us in because of this quest. Christ comes to set us free from this. To have our identity and worth and joy from Him.

Nourishing Our Souls with God's Truth

How are we to balance our Instagram feed of seemingly perfect people with our own insecurities? How can we be secure in Christ when our dark roots are showing? Can I get an amen? We have separated our faith in Jesus from the rest of our identity. We believe in God, but do we *believe* God? Do we believe His promises to us and about us? Do we even know them? We may be familiar with the current week's issue of *People* magazine, but are we familiar with the Word of God? There is power in reading God's Word daily.

We live in a world full of spiritually dead people. What else is there to care for besides looks, money, power, and status when your soul is dead and focused only on your own selfish ambition? Yet all those pursuits lead to death. We need to be feeding our souls with Scripture so that we don't buy into the things that will pass away.

Romans 4:17 says, "God . . . gives life to the dead and calls into being things that were not." Let's claim this promise over our lives, friends! Let's commit to having minds that aren't dead but are alive and thriving for things that are of eternal importance.

Colossians 3:3 tells us, "For you died, and your life is now hidden with Christ in God." We are walking among the dead yet we have a different mind-set. Our focus is on Christ, and His light radiates from our beings. That is the life we were made for.

Remembering What Jesus Values

I am in my midthirties, and in many ways this is the prime of my life physically. I know and am secure with who I am. So many insecurities of my teenage and twentysomething years are a thing of my past. However, I also am starting to see crow's-feet around my eyes and wrinkles on my face. Beauty is a never-ending battle. When you are young you have so much time on your hands you constantly examine yourself in the mirror and every imperfection is magnified. Then, when you get a little more grounded and confident in yourself, your body starts to age! It is a cruel cycle. The quest for perfection in beauty never ends. You will constantly be running.

Beth Moore, in her book *Breaking Free*, describes our minds as rooms that we have wallpapered with lies. And so we need to revamp things a little. We need to memorize Scripture and the promises God gives us. We need to remember and remind ourselves where our identity lies. Focus on the person Christ created us to be. We need to paint over that wallpaper in our hearts with truth. To do that we need to know what the truth is, and then remind ourselves daily. We are being reminded daily about what the culture values, so we need to go up against that with what Jesus values.[4]

Before Amanda Bynes started getting into the trouble she is currently in, she was in a cute, teenybopper movie called *What a Girl Wants*. In the movie, her Prince Charming said a beautiful quote: "Why are you trying so hard to fit in when you were born to stand out?"[5]

According to God's promises, you and I were made at this point of time in history, in this area, with our own specific personality. We are called to be mirrors of Christ. The way you laugh, your sense of humor, and the glimmer in your eye were designed by God to reflect Him, at this moment, in this world right now. And you are insecure about the fact that your eyes are brown? You wanted green eyes? How absurd does that sound when you put it in the context of eternity? Your purpose is to give God's invisible character a glimpse of visibility—by being who He created you to be. Be secure and bold in yourself and give glory to God through your life.

When we feel insecure, we are basically telling the Lord that we know better. His Word declares that He created us, loves us, and is pleased by us. He designed all our qualities and placed us right here, right now, for His purpose. And we complain that our hair is wavy. If only we could have straight hair. When we do that, we are telling God that we are not pleased with His plan and that we somehow have a better idea. We somehow think our lives are all about us, for our own selfish desire and plans. This couldn't be further from the truth. We are made to reflect the Lord. Our lives are designed to point people to Jesus.

We matter to Jesus. If you took a one-hundred-dollar bill and held it up to give away, everyone in the room would want it. If you crumpled it up and stepped on it, everyone would still gladly accept that hundred-dollar bill. Even if it is dirty, people still want it. We are the same in God's eyes. Our decisions, our actions, and our dress size don't affect our value in Jesus' eyes. We are infinitely valuable to the Maker of the universe. Do we really believe that? We may know that in our heads, but do our actions and words reflect that we experience it in our hearts?

I love the verse that says, "The eyes of the Lord search the whole earth in order to strengthen those whose hearts are fully committed to him" (2 Chronicles 16:9 NLT). The eyes of the Lord are searching to and fro, all over the world. God wants to involve us in His plan of redeeming the world, and He wants to give us strength when He calls us on this adventure. His eyes are scanning the earth, inviting us into this eternal adventure. If our minds are distracted and sidetracked, we will never be used in the way He desires for us. We must pay attention to what we are focused on and take control of our thought life.

Comparing Ourselves to Others

My girlfriends and I have shared a funny observation we see in some women. Many times, we have noticed, women dress for other women. I mean, let's be honest: my husband doesn't care if the soles of my shoes are red. But you know who cares about that? Other women. And if a man cares, it's probably because a woman has trained him to notice such things. Women check out other women way more than men check out women. A man will give a quick glance, but women size each other up.

I used to know more about the outfit of a woman who walked by us than any guy in the room. I would look her up and down and somehow determine—what? Her value? Then I started paying attention to my thoughts regarding other women. Some of my "checking out" is fine. I like looking at makeup tricks and fashion. I am a girlie girl, what can I say? But some of my thoughts were competitive in nature. I was sizing myself up against other women based on their appearance. Why? Who cares? I am losing no matter what when I play this dangerous game with my thoughts.

Through social media, I have a lot of followers who don't know me personally but are perhaps fans or even "love to hate me" types. I could post the most beautiful picture of myself and someone will point out a flaw. Someone always responds with a rude, mean comment. Why? Does that make them feel better about themselves? I don't know. I don't even know these people, but it seems they have a despair within that just overflows from them.

What is it within us that wants to tear each other down? When we see someone doing well or experiencing success in some way, why do we want to take away a bit of that from them? Matthew 12:34 says, "For the mouth speaks what the heart is full of." What we say is an overflow of our hearts, and in social media what we post is an overflow of our souls. If we are encouraging and complimentary toward others, then we are most likely feeling that way inside.

Stay in Your Lane

When we are resting our identity in Jesus, there is no competition. We really do desire good for one another. We want others to have the hope and love that we have in Jesus. Our love for Christ is not like any other relationship because we want others to know and love Him like we do. Since we have experienced such great love and acceptance, we want everyone around us to have the wholeness we now feel.

My husband and I often tell each other, "Stay in your lane." This is an expression we use to remind the other that we are on a path. It doesn't matter where the car next to us is going, how fast it is going, or even what kind of car it is. We are in our own lane and we know where we are going. We need to stay in our lane and focus on ourselves. There will always be someone prettier, smarter, blonder, skinnier, whatever-ier. Who cares? What does that have to do with you? Stay in your lane. Focus on your journey, for your journey is great!

Discussion Guide

- Describe a time in your life when you felt beautiful.
- How do you feel about the world's concept of beauty and the pursuit of perfection? Are you chasing after these things in your own life?
- Lydia gives an example of women checking out other women. Do you have an example when you have experienced this firsthand? How did that make you feel?
- Matthew 12:34 says, "For the mouth speaks what the heart is full of." Are you aware of the words that you use and the positivity or negativity that comes out of your mouth? As you take an inventory of your words, what do they reveal to you about the state of your soul?
- Lydia mentions the quote, "Why are you trying hard to fit in when you were born to stand out?" What does that mean to you?
- Write down Psalm 139:14: "I praise you because I am fearfully and wonderfully made; your works are wonderful, I know that full well." Put this verse in your car or on the bathroom mirror. Make a conscious effort to remind yourself of how God sees you.

eleven

Confident Lady

It takes courage to grow up and
become who you really are.
—*E. E. Cummings*

E VERYONE WHO KNOWS my mother loves her. She not
only marches to the beat of her own drum, but she
conducts a totally different orchestra then most people
walk to. She has always been this way. When I was in sixth
grade, we had recently moved from Canada to California
and I still wasn't sure of where or how I fit in. There was a
charity event held once a year, where all the mothers and
daughters would have brunch together and socialize. A
few of my new friends told me about the event, and my
mom and I got the invitation to attend the brunch.

My mom wore an angel jacket with flowers made of sequins and bright colors. Yes, it was the eighties, but most moms there were in cardigans and pearls. We entered the room, and we definitely stood out. In a sea of sameness, I was holding my mom's hand and I could feel all eyes on us, almost as a spotlight shining on our visible oddness.

I will always remember the confidence my mother displayed that day. She was sure of herself. She felt beautiful in that sequined angel jacket, and she was rocking her own personal style. I don't know if I ever was prouder to be her daughter. We were not invited to be part of that charity club, but I was invited, through my mom's example that day, into a life of confidence. It doesn't matter what everyone else is wearing or thinking. You are a star and born to shine as brightly as you can, in whatever way you feel. We can be confident in our uniqueness, not in the pursuit of perfection.

God created us all. We are all unique but connected through the notion that we all magnify God's beauty. Our worth is based on being created in His image, not Victoria Secret's image. Yet somehow there is this notion inside my head that tells me if I put the perfect outfit on the perfect body, then I will be more beautiful and, therefore, have more worth.

"Yet I Am Lovely"

In Song of Solomon 1:5, Solomon's wife says, "Dark am I, yet lovely, daughters of Jerusalem." This verse mentions the thing she would have been the most insecure about according to her culture: the darkness of her skin. In her society, dark skin was not desirable; it was a means of insecurity. Dark skin in that day meant you were in the working class, working in the sun all day. Yet Solomon's wife doesn't bow down to that idea. She fears the Lord more then she fears her culture. So she says, "Dark am I, yet lovely . . ."

I want to be the type of woman who admits her own insecurities but doesn't compromise her confidence and identity because of them! I am still lovely although I am several pounds overweight, am getting wrinkles, have brown spots . . . and on and on I could go in my mind. But no, the list will stop! "Yet I am lovely."

I am lovely because my worth isn't determined by my dress size or dress label. I am lovely because I am fearfully and wonderfully made (Psalm 139:14). I am lovely because I have the seal of the Holy Spirit on me (Ephesians 4:30). I am lovely because I belong to my Master and have been bought with a price (1 Corinthians 6:20).

Confidence in Our Value

Our magazine, *Beverly Hills Lifestyle,* tries to focus on stories that show the triumph of the human spirit. Doug and I have gotten to do all sorts of travel reviews and crazy adventures because of the magazine. One time we interviewed Kris Jenner, and she said her favorite quote was from Proverbs: "She is clothed with strength and dignity; she can laugh at the days to come" (Proverbs 31:25).

Regardless of what you think about the Kardashian family, Kris Jenner was quoting wise advice from the ancient text of Proverbs. Each of us knows and yearns for true beauty. I pray we all can have such confidence in who we are in Christ that we can be clothed in strength and dignity and laugh at the future, for nothing can shake us from the love we have for Jesus.

Our thoughts about who we are matter. Sometimes I am baffled about what I will let cross my mind about myself. I need to stop myself in my tracks and cling to the promises of Christ. I need to have confidence. If you don't think you can, you won't. The same is true about believing in the worth and beauty within yourself. The woman from Song of Solomon knew that her skin was dark, but she also knew she was beautiful and confident. It's ironic because nowadays, in our Western culture, having a tan shows you have time to bask in the sun and it is desirable and considered beautiful. You can even get a fake spray tan. Our society's expectations play into our psyche more than we realize.

Heirs to the Highest Throne

Society's concept of beauty changes. The color of your skin, the size of your swimsuit—it doesn't matter what society says. Plus, society will probably be changing its ideas in a few years. We've gone from skinny eyebrows to bushy eyebrows, skinny jeans to flared bottoms. Fashion standards are constantly in flux.

But our true beauty is defined by our Maker. He says we are beautiful, always, no matter what the current trends are. He says we belong to Him, and He thinks we are valuable and lovely.

We are all royalty. We have a King as our Father, and that makes us princesses. You are royalty. Feel like it. Think of how the world puts Britain's Princess Kate on a pedestal. Her every outfit is documented for the world to see. She is heir to a worldly throne, but we are heirs to a throne that will last for eternity.

Romans 8:17 says, "Now if we are children, then we are heirs—heirs of God and co-heirs with Christ, if indeed we share in his sufferings in order that we may also share in his glory." Have confidence in this and live your life accordingly. Let's live like we believe we are heirs to the highest throne in all creation! We need to be mindful of this. We are bombarded with a different way of thinking every day and so we have to be deliberate about telling ourselves the truth.

We need to think about what we think about. We have to guard our minds and remind ourselves that we have worth. We are wonderful and full of sparkle. Of course the enemy wants to tear us down, because we can be used for such grand things to glorify the Lord—and if we doubt ourselves, we never will believe we can be used for all God has planned for us.

In John 8:31–32 Jesus says, "If you hold to my teaching, you are really my disciples. Then you will know the truth, and the truth will set you free."

We need to work at this, ladies. If we know Jesus and we read His Word regularly, then we will experience lives of freedom. We don't just believe in Christ one afternoon on a retreat and then sit back and watch as the rest of life falls into place. Your salvation happens in a moment, but your experiences of the Holy Spirit are on-going. Constant contentment is something we all must work toward every day of our lives.

Seeing God As He Really Is

In her book *Lies Women Believe*, Nancy Leigh DeMoss says, "One of the areas that is particularly impacted by our view of God is our view of ourselves. If we do not see Him as He really is—if we believe things about Him that are not true—invariably, we will have a distorted view of ourselves."[1]

Do we see God as He really is? I have always struggled with the concept of our identity in Christ and what that really looks like in a tangible way. But to have our identity rooted in Christ, we must know and believe Christ. Many times we think we believe God, but our actions or thoughts prove that we are still seated on the throne of our minds. In our thinking, God is like a spare tire for us, there in case things go awry—then we will turn to Him.

In 1 Corinthians 9:24–27, the apostle Paul says, "Do you not know that in a race all the runners run, but only one receives the prize? So run that you may obtain it. Every athlete exercises self-control in all things. They do it to receive a perishable wreath, but we an imperishable. So I do not run aimlessly; I do not box as one beating the air. But I discipline my body and keep it under control, lest after preaching to others I myself should be disqualified" (ESV).

Paul is encouraging us to have self-control. He is telling us not to run aimlessly but to be mindful. Pay attention to what you are reading, to the images you are allowing into your mind and soul. Our prize waits for us—and that includes not only eternity with Jesus but our prize is also here and now: to be set free from the bondage and the aimless, never-ending quest for perfection.

Value Beyond Physical Appearance

I love looking in Scripture for clues to Jesus' appearance and what He looked like. Of course we all have seen drawings and images of Him, but I like to let my mind wander and really picture His face in my mind.

Isaiah 53:2 tells us that Jesus was normal looking: "He had no beauty or majesty to attract us to him, nothing in his appearance that we should desire him." There was nothing in Jesus' physical appearance that would draw people to Him. His identity was in His Father, and that was what changed the world.

I love this! I look up to so many women whom I see as the most magnificent ladies, yet from the world's point of view their physical appearance is just average. But to me, as they speak wisdom over me and walk with me through life, they shine like bright stars. That is the kind of beauty Jesus possessed, and it's the kind of value and beauty each of us can attain as we grow in knowledge of God and spend time in His presence.

First Peter 2:4 says that we come to Jesus, "the living Stone—rejected by humans but chosen by God and precious to him." Jesus was rejected by people, yet He was chosen by and precious to God. God is what gave Jesus, and us, our value. Our worth is not based on other people's opinions of us or any other outer accolades. In the end, and really every day leading up to the end, all we should focus on is that we are precious to God. We can rest in full assurance that we matter to our Maker. We are chosen by Him, and that makes us very attractive.

Confidence That Will Last

If we are basing our relationships on beauty, then as we age and our physical beauty starts to fade, so will our relationships. My husband thinks I am beautiful, but we are connected on so many levels other than physical attraction. We are best friends and love to share our lives together. He prays for me and desires to protect and encourage me and I him. If our entire relationship were based only on our outward appearances, our relationship would end. We are growing older. Our bodies are changing. I definitely don't look the same way I did when Doug and I met at age twenty-one! Yikes.

Life is too short to waste, especially on something as fleeting as physical appearance. It is important we develop our souls and focus on things that will last. We must invest in the things that are good, noble, and true. We are spiritual beings having a physical experience. Our bodies were not meant to last forever.

Philippians 4:8 encourages us, "Whatever is true, whatever is noble, whatever is right, whatever is pure, whatever is lovely, whatever is admirable—if anything is excellent or praiseworthy—think about such things." Let's make that our prayer, friends. Be mindful of your mind and hold up your thoughts to this standard. We are all princesses, so let's act like it!

Discussion Guide

- Proverbs 31:25 says, "She is clothed with strength and dignity; she can laugh at the days to come." What does it mean to be "clothed with strength and dignity"? Can you think of someone who is a great example of this type of woman?

- Read Philippians 4:8 out loud. Do your thoughts reflect the characteristics in this list? What in your thought life doesn't measure up to this list? What are you going to do about it?

- What is something you can do in your daily life that would help you remember that your identity is in Jesus and not in your appearance?

- Lydia writes, "We are all royalty. We have a King as our Father, and that makes us princesses. You are royalty. Feel like it. . . . We are heirs to a throne that will last for eternity." How do you feel about this concept of being royalty? Do you feel like God's heir? How can we live this out in our daily lives?

- Have you ever thought about Jesus' physical appearance before? Does it free you in any way to know that Jesus was not the most handsome man to walk the earth?

- "Dark am I, yet lovely," says Solomon's wife in Song of Solomon 1:5. What is it about yourself that brings you insecurities? Say or write down: "____ am I, yet lovely." Train your mind to be assured of this truth.

twelve

Forgiveness

> If you judge people, you have no
> time to love them.
> —*Mother Teresa*

I BECAME A CHRISTIAN at a Young Life camp my freshman year of high school. Every summer my youth group would take around twenty-five high schoolers to summer camp for the week. My freshman year I decided to go . . . mostly because my friends were going.

That summer we went to a camp called Malibu. It is located in Canada and is beautiful. When I think about that summer, I just smile and my heart is full of happy, peaceful, warm memories.

My closest friends growing up included Denise and Kristin. We did everything together. They were like sisters to me. We even had a friendship verse: "Though one may be overpowered, two can defend themselves. A cord of three strands is not quickly broken" (Ecclesiastes 4:12).

Denise, Kristin, and I encouraged each other in our walks with Jesus. They were my first friendships that were rooted and established in Christ.

Once we graduated high school and all went our separate ways for college, we vowed to stay in touch and as close as we were throughout high school. We would drive to each other's colleges to visit and called each other regularly. Over the years, friendships seem to shift and grow, either together or apart. But we knew our friendship was different and we would always remain as tight as sisters.

After college I moved to a different area and found myself closer in proximity to Denise. I found she was always a bit busy and when we would hang out, she seemed distant. Our friendship had changed and she seemed to be pulling away from me. I was very hurt by this and didn't understand what was going on. Had I done something wrong? Was Denise mad at me? Why did she seem so distant?

I did what every normal red-blooded girl would do: I decided I would talk about it . . . with someone else. I called Kristin and tried to pry answers from her.

"Has Denise said anything to you? Have I hurt her in some way? Did I do something to offend her?"

Poor Kristin. Looking back, I really should have talked to Denise directly. I couldn't understand why it seemed she had just outgrown our friendship.

As you can imagine, I was hurt and confused. These feelings quickly turned into anger. How could Denise be mad at me and just throw our friendship aside and not even have the nerve to tell me why? I would think through the past weeks and months of encounters and hang-out sessions. I would replay them over and over in my mind and get angrier and angrier with her.

The anger turned into bitterness. Old high school friends would ask me how Denise and Kristin were doing, and I would feel my stomach drop whenever I heard Denise's name.

Kristin and I would tiptoe around the issue whenever we chatted. If I knew they were seeing each other, I could tell it put poor Kristin in a horrible predicament—right smack in the middle of Denise's and my rift.

One day, I was driving with Doug to see a movie and I was feeling sorry for myself and pouring out to him my bitterness about Denise. Doug simply asked why I hadn't forgiven her yet. He actually said it more like, "You still haven't forgiven her?"

I don't recall what movie we saw that night, but I remember sitting in the movie theater, releasing Denise from my anger and forgiving her. I still don't understand what happened, though looking back I realize she must have had a good reason for the change in our friendship. But at the time, I decided that I wasn't going to carry it around with me anymore. I had to let it go. By holding on to it, I was being affected. My perception of what happened between us still had power over me. By forgiving her, I wasn't justifying or agreeing with the way she handled the situation, but I was taking away the power of her actions to affect me.

The Consequences of Unforgiveness

Forgiveness is such a hard thing to do. We often choose to be bitter at someone even though we know that the bitterness will have nothing but a negative effect on our own lives. Unforgiveness makes us angry. It can affect our physical bodies, causing us to have headaches or ulcers or even sometimes more serious ailments. We can become emotionally unstable because we have allowed a grudge to fester within us. Unforgiveness can do nothing but destroy us.

In *Living Beyond Yourself,* Beth Moore writes a beautiful paragraph that has stuck with me since the day I read it:

The Greek word most often used in the New Testament for *forgive* is *aphiemi.* It means, "to let go from one's power, possession, to let go free, let escape." In essence, the intent of biblical forgiveness is to cut someone loose. The word picture drawn by the Greek terms for unforgiveness is one in which the "unforgiven" is roped to the back of the unforgiving. How ironic. Unforgiveness is the means by which we securely bind ourselves to that which we hate most. Therefore, the Greek meaning of forgiveness might best be demonstrated as the practice of cutting loose the person roped to your back.[1]

When I read this paragraph, I couldn't help but picture all the people I hold grudges against, all the people in my life I blame for this and for that. All the people from *The Real Housewives of Orange County* reunion I had been carrying around on my back. The list of offenses against me that I go over and over in my head.

(Am I the only one?) All the things I wish I would have said to her, or ideas of how I would handle him next time . . . Beth Moore's image of all these people being roped onto my back was truth spoken into my soul. No wonder I feel like I'm drowning sometimes. I am carrying the load of four or five other people strapped onto me! I know it is right for me to forgive them, if not for them but for my own peace of mind.

Luke 11:4 says, "Forgive us our sins, for we also forgive everyone who sins against us." No one is perfect, and we have all hurt people in ways we may not even be aware of. The Lord knows that the unforgiveness trapped inside of us will only hurt us.

I can't imagine some of the wrongs that have been done to you. This world can be dark, and forgiveness can be nothing short of a miracle. But mercy is at the root of forgiveness. You aren't justifying the other person's actions by your forgiveness. You are allowing yourself to not be hurt or in bondage because of that person anymore. You are handing the pain over to Jesus and declaring that the person who hurt you will no longer have an effect on you.

However, sometimes we can grow so used to the pain that it is hard to let go of it. In some dysfunctional way the pain is the only thing we can hold on to, and letting go of it seems terrifying. Christ can handle you and the pain. When you forgive, you are giving that person over to God. Let's ask for Jesus to shine in the cracks of our soul where we have held on to unforgiveness.

Remember your past but consider your future. God desires us to be set free. We don't have to carry that guilt or shame or anger or resentment anymore. Instead, we hand them over to Christ. Those shackles don't belong on our lives anymore. Let the offense go, and be set free!

Everyone experiences pain in different ways. In John 16:33, God says, "In this world you will have trouble. But take heart! I have overcome the world." Our pain is not the end of our story. Our pain doesn't define us. We serve a God who has overcome the world, and with that, He has overcome the darkness of your hurt. Let's live in that freedom, friends!

Getting Justice Is God's Job

Mark 11:25 says, "If you hold anything against anyone, forgive them, so that your Father in heaven may forgive you your sins." We each have to give an account before our Lord. What is going on in your heart is between you and God. If someone has wronged you, God knows and sees—but it is not our job to get justice. That is God's duty.

I believe many times we think that getting justice for an offense is our job, not God's job. We want to take matters into our own hands. In all honesty, it feels good to just tell someone off, especially if we feel they deserve it because they have wronged us in some way. Maybe someone cuts us off on the freeway, or maybe a friend betrays us. We want people to know that we have been slighted and we won't stand for it!

What good does that serve, though? If we respond to being hurt by causing hurt to another person, we are then put into that mind-set and brought down to a lower level. Letting another driver know they cut us off and we are upset about it does nothing to elevate our state of mind. It spins us into self-centeredness where are we are in no way bringing light into the world.

The Bible says that God will not give us more then we can handle (1 Corinthians 10:13). When every-thing seems to be going wrong, be flattered that God knows you can handle so much! It is during our times of weakness we know that God, and only God, is working through us. He will meet us where we are and always provide a way for us to be obedient to Him.

The Humility of Forgiveness

Many times unforgiveness is really a matter of pride. We believe we have certain rights and if someone steps on our rights, we get upset. I found this clear as night and day while filming *Housewives*.

One day I came home very upset after a day of filming. But then I realized my anger was just a matter of pride. The other Housewives had slighted me, and they got away with it! They were sneaky and cunning, and I didn't want to stand for that. I thought they needed to be held accountable for their actions.

I made a conscious decision that I wasn't responsible for their actions and it wasn't my job to bring them to justice. The truth is, I am going to be held accountable solely for myself and for what I do. I decided to act justly as best I could and leave the rest up to the Lord. My *Housewives* castmates were His responsibility, not mine. It is my job to love; it is the Holy Spirit's job to convict.

In no way am I saying that I was perfect while filming the show. I have learned from the many mistakes I made and have grown deeply through my experiences on and off set. God led me to my knees many times, and I have had to look at my actions and the root of many of my shortcomings. One reason I grew so much in my spiritual walk during that time is that I looked within myself instead of pointing the finger constantly at everyone around me. I was able to take a personal inventory of my shortcomings, ask God for forgiveness, and grow from my mistakes. If I had been consumed by everyone else's actions, I never would have had the time for reflection. John 8:7 illustrates this point. Jesus said, "Let any one of you who is without sin be the first to throw a stone at her."

Many people talk about forgiving others, but not a lot of time is focused on forgiving oneself. Even more interesting is that the Bible never talks about forgiving ourselves. Yet I know many men and women who live in shame. Many have grown accustomed to guilt and live in bondage to past mistakes or actions that they regret but just can't move past.

I may not be able to find a direct verse about forgiving ourselves, but Scripture says you are forgiven. Living a life in shame or regret is not what God has planned for you. His Word declares:

- Love and faithfulness meet together; righteousness and peace kiss each other. (Psalm 85:10)

- Their sins and lawless acts I will remember no more. (Hebrews 10:17)
- As far as the east is from the west, so far has he removed our transgressions from us. (Psalm 103:12)

There are many more verses on forgiveness; in fact, the entire Bible is the story of God redeeming His people back to Himself. That's why I couldn't find specific verses on forgiving ourselves; it is the breath of Scripture! When we live in a place of shame and darkness, we are being influenced by the devil. That is not pleasing to God or God's desire for your life. Self-loathing is another form of self-centeredness.

We must remember that we are forgiven and move forward. We must believe Isaiah 1:18: "Though your sins are like scarlet, they shall be as white as snow; though they are red as crimson, they shall be like wool." We must believe that truth in our soul and cling to it. No matter what we have done, God sees us as white as snow because of Jesus. For that we can praise Him and live in freedom all the days of our lives.

I believe once we live in this freedom of grace and light and love, we will then be changed to forgive others. When people cut us off on the freeway, the offense will not get under our skin as much. We will be so focused on the kingdom of heaven that the small things will not matter to us as much. They will no longer control our spirit.

Let's agree to lighten our load and unstrap that dead weight of unforgiveness that we've been carrying around. We are not saying that the way we've been treated or wronged is okay; we are just saying we have a God we trust and He will handle it for us. It is our job to have a future of great adventure and glory for God, and we can't climb this mountain before us while carrying past bitterness on our backs. So let's choose to let go and let God!

Discussion Guide

- What are two qualities about yourself that you like and are proud of?
- Do you struggle with forgiveness in your life? Do you feel your inner peace is being destroyed by other people's actions? What can you do to make sure your peace comes from Jesus?
- Have you ever asked for forgiveness from someone and they wouldn't forgive you? How did that make you feel?
- Read John 8:7, where Jesus said, "Let any one of you who is without sin be the first to throw a stone at her." How is God moving in your heart about being judgmental?
- Do you feel forgiven, or are you carrying around a heavy load of guilt? What is your response to God's words of forgiveness, recorded in Hebrews 10:17: "Their sins and lawless acts I will remember no more"?
- Read Luke 7:36–50. This is a story of a sinner who came to Jesus and sought His forgiveness. When the Pharisee questioned her worthiness, Jesus says the beautiful response recorded in Luke 7:47: "Her

many sins have been forgiven—as her great love has shown. But whoever has been forgiven little loves little." What does this verse mean to you? What do you think He was explaining?

- Write down the name of one person who is still strapped to your back because you haven't forgiven them. Commit to asking God to help you forgive them, knowing that your forgiveness doesn't justify their actions, but it frees you.

thirteen

Finding Peace

Union with God is the only heaven
there is, and it begins here on
earth.
—*Macrina Wiederkehr*

W HEN I WAS struggling and praying about whether
to do season 9 of *The Real Housewives of Orange
County*, I asked people to pray that I would have a peace
about it. I remember tossing and turning at night, knowing the deadline was approaching and I had to make a
decision. I prayed and prayed that God would reveal His
will to me.

One morning I met with my mentor for coffee. It
was five days before I had to give my final answer to

Bravo, and I was agonizing over God's will and feeling the pressure of having to make this decision. Noelle, my mentor, looked at me and said, "I don't think God cares if you turn right or you turn left. I think He cares about the intention of the turn."

That notion was so freeing to me. There was no one, single "right" answer. It was more about my heart. Why was I making the decision? What was the root of my desire?

God cares about our hearts. He will accomplish His will, and if we are open and available to be used, then that is a blessing. As a Ugandan priest once said to me, "God is more concerned about His will than you are in following it."

Jesus Can Set Us Free

In Luke 4, we read of Jesus' first teaching in the synagogue. If you are not familiar with this story I suggest you read it, for it is wonderful! Jesus went into the synagogue and read part of Isaiah 61, which says, "The Spirit of the Sovereign Lord is on me, because the Lord has anointed me to proclaim good news to the poor. He has sent me to bind up the brokenhearted, to proclaim freedom for the captives and release from darkness for the prisoners, to proclaim the year of the LORD's favor" (vv. 1–2).

Picture this scene in your mind. Just like we do in churches across the world today, Jesus stood up in the synagogue and read the Word of God aloud to the congregation as part of the weekly service. It was His first public sermon. By the way, not coincidentally, the book of Isaiah contains more prophecy about Christ than any other.

Jesus read the Scripture passage from Isaiah 61 and then declared, according to Luke 4:21, "Today this scripture is fulfilled in your hearing." Talk about a powerful church service!

Jesus is declaring that He has come to set us free! He has come not just to save us from eternal death but also to give us life, starting today. Believing in Him doesn't mean we now have a list of rules to follow to get into heaven; it means our lives have been set free. We are now free of the fear of failure, brokenness, and heartache.

If we live a life with Jesus we are set free today, right now. Jesus is proclaiming that the Spirit of the Lord is upon Him and He has come to share the good news! He has come to set the captives free! *To set us free.* I'm not sure what chains you have around you holding your soul captive, but your Lord and Savior proclaimed that He came to set you free! Our chains hold nothing compared to Him.

Think of the story in Acts 12:1–8, when the apostle Paul was in jail. God intervened, and the chains fell off Paul's wrist so he could walk out of prison. So can we, friends! What a good word. God can cause our chains to fall off us. We don't have to live as prisoners anymore!

In Matthew 11:30, Jesus says, "My yoke is easy and my burden is light." To fully understand what Jesus is saying, we must understand His culture. In that day, you could tell which rabbi a person was following by the set of rules that person was under. A rabbi would tell his followers to obey the Ten Commandments, but then he would also add on his own set of rules, which was referred to as that teacher's "yoke." Jesus is telling us that His set of rules is not an extra burden. He is the Prince of Peace and wants to set us free. His yoke is easy and His burden is light. That was mind-boggling in His culture at that time. While other teachers were adding more and more burdens, our Savior came to make our burden light and to tear off our chains so we could freely glorify God. He wants to give us peace and freedom, not another checklist to make us feel guilty for underperforming.

The Secret of Satisfaction

Having salvation in Jesus isn't the same thing as having satisfaction. We must seek to find satisfaction. Paul says it this way in Philippians 4:12: "I know what it is to be in need, and I know what it is to have plenty. I have learned the secret of being content in any and every situation, whether well fed or hungry, whether living in plenty or in want." We must seek our satisfaction, our peace, our contentment. It is not something that comes naturally to us.

On the contrary, it is in our nature to focus on what we don't have, causing us to feel dissatisfaction. In college we focus on getting married. When we are married we want to have kids. Once we have kids, then we start thinking about sending them to school. It is in our nature to look for and want the next phase of life. Contentment is something we must learn.

Psalm 62:5–6 says, "Yes, my soul, find rest in God; my hope comes from him. Truly he is my rock and my salvation; he is my fortress, I will not be shaken."

Think about this verse. Jesus is where our hope comes from. He is where our peace is. No matter what storm we find ourselves in, our Lord is unwavering and unchanging.

Many times in a situation we let our emotions take over. We lose our sense of peace because we are living in a reality that hasn't even happened yet. We are so worried about all the things that could go wrong or will go wrong that we lose the joy of the present.

God is our answer. He is all knowing and ever present. He knows when we sit and when we stand (Psalm 139:2). He knows what we are going through. He is our peace in the storm and strength when we have nothing left to give.

When I am trying to have peace about a decision I remind myself to give my emotions time to cool down first. When we make decisions based on our emotions, we usually make the wrong call. We are deciding to do things because emotionally we want something, but it is unhealthy for us in the end. God specializes in a future and a hope. We need to remind ourselves of that. If we are walking with the Lord and are leaning into Him daily, He will give us "the peace . . . which transcends all understanding" (Philippians 4:7).

We must always remember who our God is:

- He is never changing. "I the LORD do not change" (Malachi 3:6).
- He is good. "Give thanks to the LORD, for he is good" (Psalm 136:1).
- He created us. "The LORD . . . created you" (Isaiah 43:1).
- He loves us. "This is love, not that we loved God, but that he loved us" (1 John 4:10).

If our concept of God is based on our situations, then He is changing because our circumstances are always changing. We think, *Today was a good day so God must love me.* But God is the same no matter what kind of day we are having! That can give us a sense of peace, because we have a Father in heaven who is consistent and never changing. I don't know about you, but I need a God like that!

Let's expect God to speak to us, friends. In our lives Jesus stands beside us during every conversation and every e-mail and text. God is there, waiting for us to give Him glory with our lives. The circumstances we are in may not change, but the One we're walking with through the trial is our heavenly Father, and that gives us a peace that is beyond understanding.

Peace Comes Through Prayer

As we walk through the storms of life, I want to live a life of prayer. Our goal is to be in constant communion with the Father, so why not speak to Him throughout the day? We don't pray as a means to an end; prayer is the end in itself. Like the saying goes, "If you are going to worry, don't pray, and if you're going to pray, don't worry."

- Call to me and I will answer you and tell you great and unsearchable things you do not know. (Jeremiah 33:3)
- I will climb up to my watchtower and stand at my guardpost. There I will wait to see what the LORD says and how he will answer my complaint. (Habakkuk 2:1 NLT)
- But as for me, I watch in hope for the LORD, I wait for God my Savior; my God will hear me. (Micah 7:7)

Expect God to speak to you! He not only speaks to us through prayer, but He also speaks though songs, through other people, through signs, through nature, and through our life circumstances. We are spiritual beings having a physical experience, and God uses both our spirit and our experiences in this world to connect to Him.

Sometimes we don't hear God's answer to our prayers because we aren't quiet enough to hear Him. And sometimes He is answering our prayers—but in a way we don't expect.

As I was preparing for this book, I went back and read some of my old high school journals. Oh boy! I can't begin to describe to you how relieved and happy I am that God said no to many of my teenage prayers. For example, I prayed and prayed that I would marry a particular boy. I praise my Maker that He said no to that prayer, because He knew that He had made Doug for me. At the time I saw it as unanswered prayer, but now I see God was answering—His answer was just, *Wait, I've got someone who's a better fit for you.*

Peace That Overcomes Doubt

I love the story of John the Baptist in prison. I don't love the fact that he was in prison, but I can relate to the doubt John felt while he was there. John was a prophet who dedicated his entire life to declaring to everyone that Jesus was the Messiah. That was what God had put John the Baptist on earth to do. I assume John was more familiar than anyone else at that time with all the prophecies of the coming Messiah and how Jesus fulfilled them all. John's mind knew the truth, and his eyes had seen many of Jesus' miracles. John had heard the voice of God declaring Jesus to be His Son at Jesus' baptism. John knew, he saw, and he heard. Yet he still wound up in jail.

I imagine stories were swirling around about Jesus healing a woman and bringing a boy back from the dead. Perhaps John was wondering, *If Jesus does miracles for other people, then why doesn't He rescue me?* Not only was John a prophet, but he was also Jesus' cousin. As John was sitting in prison worried for his life, he was struggling to make sense of all this.

Scripture tells us that these great people of faith were human and had doubts and frustrations and insecurities like you and I do. That is what is so fascinating and real about the Bible. God used imperfect, doubtful people. John was afraid and uncertain, so he sent his disciples to ask Jesus in Luke 7:20, "Are you the one who is to come, or should we expect someone else?"

I don't know about you, but I've been there. I've been afraid and uncertain and full of doubt. And I've asked,

"God, how could You let this happen? God, where are You? God, why?"

Have you ever had a season in your life where everything was uncertain? It seemed your whole life was a storm and you were getting tossed about. Yet in those seasons, when we cling to Jesus, He gives us a deep kind of peace that we don't experience when everything is sunny and perfect. During those times when Jesus is all I have, I have been driven to my knees in prayer and clung to the Lover of my soul. I have an intimacy with Him that can't be found any other way, except through that painful storm. God wants our hearts, and many times He allows a storm to swirl around us so we will turn to Him as our shelter. God allows us to walk through the storms of life because He knows we will come out the other end more refined and closer to Him. We can remain peaceful in the midst of turmoil because God is big and mighty and real and with us.

"Shalom, I Love You!"

When I was in high school my youth group would go on weekend retreats a few times every year. One of my favorite moments of the retreats would be when my youth pastor, Bob Schrimpf, told the story of two believers walking on the dirt roads in Israel. When they passed one another they would look each other in the eyes and say, "Shalom." This word is a common Hebrew greeting, and it means "peace, completeness, and prosperity." So when you say, "Shalom," you are wishing the other person to have peace in a world that offers us anything but most days.

On our retreats, after Bob told us the story, we would then go around the room, look into each other's eyes and say, "Shalom, I love you!" Then we would give each other a hug. For me this was a small glimpse of heaven. We all wished each other peace, completeness, and prosperity, being filled with the Holy Spirit and encouraging one another. That brief moment represented peace on earth.

The Bible says that God is redeeming the world through us. When the world sees our peace from God that transcends all understanding, it gets a glimpse of God. Although circumstances in our lives often tempt us to freak out or worry, we can stand on solid rock and proclaim peace—not just for ourselves, but for one another. Shalom, my friends. I love you.

Discussion Guide

- What is something you do that brings you peace?
- Lydia talks about Jesus declaring that we are set free. Do you believe this? When was a time in your life you felt you had chains on you? How did you break free from that bondage?
- Do you feel Christ's yoke is easy, or do you feel overwhelmed and stressed by your ideas of Christianity?
- Would you say you are overall a contented person? What are some things you are always looking forward to that are robbing you of your present? How can you learn to be content in the here and now?
- Can you relate to John the Baptist's doubt? Have you gone through a season of doubt in your life? Have you come to terms with this or are you still struggling and holding onto bitterness?
- Lydia gave some verses supporting God's good, loving character. What is your favorite verse from the ones she shared? Commit that verse to memory.

fourteen

In the World, Not of the World

Our greatest fear . . . should not
be of failure but of succeeding
at things in life that don't really
matter.

—*Francis Chan*

LOVE A GOOD PARTY. Dressing up, celebrating, getting
people together—I'm passionate about them. As a
"Bravolebrity," a world of red carpets, fancy parties,
and free loot opens up to you. Designers want to send
you their dresses, and promoters want you to make an
appearance at their next big event.

When Doug and I were first thrown into this world,
we were driving up to Los Angeles many nights of the

week. It was fun and exciting. We were having our photo taken for weekly magazines and getting to meet all sorts of celebrities.

But after about a dozen of these events, they started to lose their appeal to us. We would be in some beautiful ballroom or hip Hollywood club, but we were longing to be at home tucking our kids into bed. I remember sitting at a booth for an *Us Weekly* "Hot 100" party. The cast members of *Dancing with the Stars* were on the dance floor, and every booth around me was filled with celebrities. It was an amazing scene, and I was smack in the middle of it. This night provided everything the world tells you makes a good night.

Our babysitter sent us a short video of our boys at home, fresh out of the bath and wearing their pajamas. There were saying good-night to Doug and me, kissing the camera and sending us their love. I got tears in my eyes watching the video. That was where my heart was. That was where I was longing to be. That was what matters and lasts.

Yes, the party was amazing, but it was just like every other party on the circuit. There will always be another party. My boys are growing quickly, and this time with them is so special. Those moments are the ones that will last. My sons will remember the routine and rhythms of their childhood. Of course it is important to deepen your relationship with your spouse and have a date night and a social life of your own, but I had lost my balance. Doug and I were becoming fixtures on the Hollywood circuit, and I didn't have my mind set on eternal things.

Are We Being Set Apart?

I put off writing this chapter for a number of reasons. I feel like the message of Christians being "in the world, not of the world" is so important for us all to hear that I don't want to miss anything. I also feel like a hypocrite when so often in my life I have had the aroma of my worldly desires all over me. But it's time for us to stop and take an honest assessment of our lives.

Do people know we are followers of Christ? Are we set apart? Are we different from people in the world? Let's think about what we wear. What we watch. The words we use. The way we spend our money.

Are there areas in our lives that don't reflect Christ? What are they reflecting? Our desire to fit in—or even to be better than others? In Galatians 1:10, the apostle Paul asks, "Am I trying to win the approval of human beings, or of God? Or am I trying to please people? If I were still trying to please people, I would not be a servant of Christ." Is this true of how we live? Our culture has made it become the norm to segment our faith away from the rest of our lives, but Christ tells us that when we give Him our whole lives then we will truly find them. He isn't only interested in our Sunday morning worship. He wants people who are sold out for Him every day.

Learn to Be Content

What does it mean to live in this world but not buy in to this world? Let's consider our culture. Everywhere we look, billboards and commercials are selling us lies. The world around us is on a journey of consumption and a never-ending quest for more.

So how do we keep ourselves from being "in the world" when it comes to this area of consumerism? We must get rid of the desire to acquire. We must learn to be content with what God has given us. We must be conscious of what we are allowing to enter our minds and be on guard.

Consumerism is only one element this world has to offer. The world also promotes success. Being first.

Getting what's yours. But these desires of our flesh are opposed to our spirits. Our hearts are deceitful. They tell us to go after things that are of no worth. We must learn to trust the Holy Spirit inside of us over our flesh.

How do we stay "in the world, not of the world" when it comes to success? We need to close our eyes to the visible and open them to the invisible God. As 2 Corinthians 4:18 says, "We fix our eyes not on what is seen, but on what is unseen, since what is seen is temporary, but what is unseen is eternal." When our quiet times become sparse and our eyes are fixed not on Jesus but on our closets, it is easy to get caught up in the world. Yet when we hold this world and all it has to offer up against our spiritual inheritance, there is no contest.

Let Your Light Shine

Please don't mishear me. This world is beautiful and magnificent. Our families and friendships and many things we experience here bring us joy and delight, as they should. We aren't called to be unattached and just wait around to be taken to Jesus. We are called to live in this world, but not buy in to its way of order. To be set apart as lights shining in darkness. Jesus said in Matthew

5:14, "You are the light of the world. A town built on a hill cannot be hidden."

We have the light of Christ radiating from us. Have you ever been around someone who just commands the room? Have you been around a believer who had the authority of God in his or her being? Perhaps that person can pray with authority and faith. Or maybe they are just calm. I know a lady whose voice is consistently calm. It's not the tone of her voice; it's what is behind it. I can tell just from her presence that she is a woman of peace. What would people say about you? Are you a light? Do you radiate light and swell with joy? (Isaiah 60:5).

John 16:33 says, "I have told you these things, so that in me you may have peace. In this world you will have trouble. But take heart! I have overcome the world." As followers of Jesus Christ, this life on earth is the closest to hell we will ever experience. We are in this world and this world affects us, and it should. But we must be mindful that we are set apart, we are lights in darkness, and we hold ourselves up to a standard that is different than the rest. Our road is narrow and not wide. Let's not allow the ways of this world to dictate what we value and cling to or to pull us down. We are called to be lights. We are to be set apart and different.

Many times if you walk into a dark room, it takes a minute for your eyes to adjust to the darkness. But if you are standing in a room and the lights slowly start to fade, you don't really notice that the light is dimming. We must be on guard with our lives! We may find ourselves in situations where we are standing in a dark room and we don't know how we got there.

Romans 6:11–14 tells us:

In the same way, count yourselves dead to sin but alive to God in Christ Jesus. Therefore do not let sin reign in your mortal body so that you obey its evil desires. Do not offer any part of yourself to sin as an instrument of wickedness, but rather offer yourselves to God as those who have been brought from death to life; and offer every part of yourself to him as an instrument of righteousness. For sin shall no longer be your master, because you are not under the law, but under grace.

As Christians, sin is not our master! We are not slaves to our desires but we have the undeserving love of God. His grace has set us free and we have no condemnation under Him! Because of Christ's love toward me I enter into a relationship with Him and He changes who I am. Who I was is now dead and I am created new because of my faith.

Renew Your Mind

We need to renew our minds (Ephesians 4:23). Renewing is a process. It is always ongoing. It doesn't just happen once, but is a deliberate act that takes place through being dedicated and set apart. Once you become your new self in God, your old ways are not your ways anymore. This doesn't mean you aren't going to struggle. It merely means it's no longer in your nature to be okay with the things you used to be okay with because the Holy Spirit now lives inside of you. However, there is a selfish part, the flesh part of you, that wants its old way and desires. This is the tension we feel every day.

God's way is so counterintuitive to what our culture has conditioned us to believe. The world says you must succeed. You must do well and do big. Yet I have met so many successful people who are empty and sad. Why do you suppose so many successful people are depressed? Having it all, whatever *it* is, is not enough. Things will never be enough. It's like that age-old expression that you have a God-shaped hole in your heart and no matter what else you try to fill that hole with, it will be empty because it's not the right shape. We need God. Pastor and author Francis Chan goes further and says, "The irony is that while God doesn't need us but still wants us, we desperately need God but don't really want Him most of the time."[1] Wow. Read that again and then fall on your knees and praise our Lord for the grace and love He bestows on us. I can't help but praise my King of kings for the great love story we are asked to be a part of.

You Are the Bride of Christ

We are the bride of Christ. He is making His appeal to the world though us, and the world is watching. Through our actions, our joy, and our patience, we bear witness to Christ. Of course we will fall and mess up, and that is where Jesus' grace comes in. We are not bound to the law of perfection and rituals anymore. We are set free to have a radical and real relationship with the Creator of the world and to live that out loud. Boldly!

I love my husband. He knows me and loves me and cherishes me. Because of him I act differently. Because he is my husband, my identity now is wrapped up in being Mrs. McLaughlin. When I was single, I had a different name and my way of life was different. Imagine if the people I came in contact with didn't know I had gotten married. They didn't know I had met Doug and fallen in love. Why would I try to hide my new relationship? How absurd does that sound? Yet many Christians live their lives like that. They fall in love with Christ, but they want to hide this new relationship instead of acting like a new creation and a changed woman! I praise God I am not the person I was before I knew Him.

Are there people in your life who have no clue you are a Christian? Maybe you have close friends or family members who don't believe but you haven't broached the subject because you feel it would be uncomfortable or awkward. Pray and seek Jesus over that situation. He may provide opportunities for you to speak boldly. He has placed you in your specific family and group of friends for a reason. None of that is coincidental. Don't miss the opportunity to be part of God moving and working.

Let's not become so consumed with the world that we are holding on to it with tightly clenched fists. We are here to glorify God and be a light. He wants to use us, but we must let Him. We simply have to open our hands and let the blessings flow from heaven. He may call us into awkward situations, or to walk away from something that could be a lot of fun and prestige, but we can know for certain that He has something better for us. Jesus says, "It won't be easy, but I promise it will be worth it."

Let's fix our eyes on the things that are eternal—on the things that really matter and have substance and meaning. None of us will be lying on our deathbed wishing we had spent more time working or at the gym. Instead, in our last moments on earth we will remember the people we met. The love we gave. The moments when we felt the Holy Spirit move us.

We are eternal beings and have eternity set in our hearts (Ecclesiastes 3:11). We are here on the earth having a wonderful adventure. Let's remind each other what really matters—and to do that we have to be in the world, not of the world!

Discussion Guide

- What is your favorite thing about this world? For example, do you love food, traveling, nature, etc.?

- Does your life reflect Christ in you? Does everyone in your life know you are a believer? Do you think you are a good portrayal of Christ's love by the way you live?

- Does your faith flow out of every part of your life, or do you tend to segment your faith away from other aspects of your life?

- Lydia talks about consumerism and our culture's desire to acquire. How does this play out in your life? Is this something you're aware of?

- Francis Chan says, "Our greatest fear . . . should not be of failure but of succeeding at things in life that don't really matter."[2] What are you putting your energy and focus into?

- In what areas of your life do you think you are still living "in the world"?

- What do you feel God is boldly calling you to do that would require you to step out in faith?

fifteen

Live Your Great Adventure

What you are is God's gift to you, what you become is your gift to God.

—*Hans Urs von Balthasar*

I N EPHESIANS 3:16–19, the apostle Paul expresses a heartfelt prayer that gives much encouragement to each of us:

I pray that out of his glorious riches he may strengthen you with power through his Spirit in your inner being, so that Christ may dwell in your hearts through faith. And I pray that you, being rooted and established in love, may have power, together with all the Lord's holy people, to grasp how wide and long and high and deep is the love of Christ, and to know this love that surpasses knowledge—that you may be filled to the measure of all the fullness of God.

What a prayer over us! As I read the apostle Paul's prayer, I am moved to my knees in tears. I want to have the power of Christ dwell in me! And in you, precious friends.

How do we experience that kind of power? The Bible says we get that through our faith.

I also want to be rooted and established in love. As a mom, I try to give my children love, love, and more love. When you know you are loved, you are bolder and more secure in yourself. I think that is why Paul prays that we would know the fullness of God's love. God loves each of us—no matter what—perfectly and divinely.

I desire to be filled by the fullness of God. And I pray that over you, my sweet friend. I pray that somehow the words and thoughts in this book would encourage you in your pursuit of our Savior. The fullness of God overflows with all things good and just and light and holy. Like Paul, I pray that God's presence would radiate and fill our beings.

We were not created to be empty, so we try to fill the void within us. Some people try to fill it with other relationships, jobs, or even family life. But the truth is, we were created by God to be inhabited by His Spirit. The vacuum in every human's life doesn't yearn to be fixed; it yearns to be filled. This is why Paul prays for us to "be filled to the measure of all the fullness of God."

Remember, your life is God's gift to you, and what you do with your life is your gift to God. You have unique talents and gifts that only you have in this moment, at this point of history. Your life is precious and a gift. Be bold, brave, mighty, and full of confidence that God is on your team and cheering you on. He is directing your plays and orchestrating your entire life.

The Time Is Now

When I was in college, I went on *Semester at Sea*. This is a big ship on which we traveled to different countries while taking classes on the boat. One of my professors on the ship was a man named Dr. Spates. Dr. Spates was around six feet tall and always reminded me of a captain. Maybe it was because we were on a ship, but he had the disposition and movements like he was the captain. He would say, "We all live once—if that." We only live once, so let's really live! This is our one chance. How sad it would be to look back on your life and feel like you never truly lived.

It is so easy to get sidetracked and focus our thoughts, actions, and life on things that are temporal and physical. We focus on our bills and our long to-do lists. Those things will bury us alive if we let them. We must be about our Father's business. Today there is enough time to complete what God desires of you today. You probably won't get everything done, but if we focus on what has eternal, kingdom worth, then we will have enough time and energy to complete our task at hand.

Be encouraged and secure and fired up. Jesus wants you to let go of the past and the burdens you carry. Second Corinthians 5:17 promises us, "Therefore, if anyone is in Christ, the new creation has come: The old has gone, the new is here!"

The time is now. You do not have to wait until you go to a zillion Bible studies or become some spiritual person you have conjured up in your mind.

Francis Chan once gave an example of how silly Christians have become. He used the backdrop of cleaning our room.[1] We know we need to clean our room, so we form a committee where we met once a week about strategies for cleaning our room. We read books about how to clean our room, and then we all sit around and talk about one day cleaning our room. How absurd would that be, yet many times that is how we view church and our relationship with Jesus. No! Go clean your room! You are equipped if you have the seal of the Holy Spirit on you. He promises to meet us and give us words when we have none. What an adventure we are called on!

We Have a Great Big God

I believe many times we don't live our lives boldly because of fear and disbelief. We are afraid that God won't come through for us, which causes us to doubt Him or maybe not even believe in Him at all.

All too often, my prayers reveal that my view of God is very small. I pray for the safety of my kids, for health and protection of my family. I don't think these are bad things to pray for, but if I fully comprehended how big and vast and powerful my Creator is, I would have bolder prayers. What do your prayers reveal about you?

When I hold my prayers up to the fullness of God and what I know about Him, I am embarrassed. Matthew 8:26 says, "You of little faith, why are you so afraid?" And that is not what I want my Savior to say about me. I want to hear, "Well done, good and faithful servant! You have been faithful with a few things; I will put you in charge of many things. Come and share your master's happiness!" (Matthew 25:21).

That is what my life needs to be about. I want my Master to look at me and say, "Well done, good and faithful servant!" I don't want Him to say, "Well, you were safe. You took no risks for Me, but hey, you were moderately happy most days, so way to go."

I now start my prayer time by focusing on God. I take time to picture who He really is. I focus on having a healthy reverence and fear of the Lord, thinking of verses that describe Him in His heavenly realm, such as:

- For the LORD your God is a consuming fire. (Deuteronomy 4:24)
- And the one who sat there had the appearance of jasper and ruby. A rainbow that shone like an emerald encircled the throne. (Revelation 4:3)
- As I looked, "thrones were set in place, and the Ancient of Days took his seat. His clothing was as white as snow; the hair of his head was white like wool. His throne was flaming with fire, and its wheels were all ablaze." (Daniel 7:9)

This is our great big God. I am praying to the Ancient of Days, and all I can muster up to ask for is continued health? Our prayer life needs to be bold and transformative.

You and I are children of God and heirs to the heavenly throne. Let's start acting like it! Don't use your thoughts to beat yourself up. Don't live in a prison of guilt. Have faith in your Maker and know that it is not too late. Trust Him and live your life as a light to this world.

Our faith journey is a grand adventure. It will be victorious and joyful, but it will also be filled with tribulation and wandering in the desert. If at times it feels like you are falling, rest assured you are falling into the arms of Jesus. And really, is there any place you would rather be?

Discussion Guide

- State one way you have been changed or a perspective you have gained while reading this book.
- Read aloud Ephesians 3:16–19. What part of that prayer stands out to you? Why? What part of that prayer would you like to see tangible in your life right now?
- Jesus says in Luke 14:33 that His disciples are to leave everything and come follow Him. In what ways have you sacrificed for your faith?
- How would you describe your prayer life? Are your prayers safe or bold? Have you seen God work in your prayer life? Has this affected the way you pray today?
- Read again the three verses describing God in heaven: Deuteronomy 4:24, Revelation 4:3, and Daniel 7:9. Were these new images for you? Is it hard for you to picture our Maker like that? Does it encourage you to pray bolder prayers?
- Do you feel a calling to a journey in your own personal life? This chapter includes a quote from Lydia's college professor, "We all live once—if that." What changes do you feel you need to make in your life to really live?

Notes

Charge to You

1. Jen Hatmaker, Deeper Conference (Rock Harbor Church, Costa Mesa, CA, May 31, 2013).

Chapter 1: Answering the Call

1. Stefanie Phan, "Sky's the Limit," *Riviera Orange County*, March 2009, 66, http://www.skylabmodernart.com/riviera_skylab.pdf.

Chapter 8: Love, Love, Love

1. C. S. Lewis, *The Four Loves* (New York: Houghton Mifflin Harcourt, 1991), 121.
2. Oswald Chambers, *He Shall Glorify Me* (Fort Washington, PA: Christian Literature Crusade, 1965), 134.

Chapter 9: Family Matters

1. Jen Hatmaker, *Out of the Spin Cycle: Devotions to Lighten Your Mother Load* (Grand Rapids: Revell, 2010), 29.

Chapter 10: Created Beautiful

1. Dove Research: *The Real Truth About Beauty: Revisited,* cited in Dove, "Surprising Self-Esteem Statistics," accessed December 29, 2014, http://www.dove.us/Social-Mission/Self-Esteem-Statistics.aspx.

2. "Statistics and Facts on the Cosmetic Industry," Statistica, accessed December 29, 2014, http://www.statista.com/topics/1008/cosmetics-industry/.

3. American Society for Aesthetic Plastic Surgery, "The American Society for Aesthetic Plastic Surgery Reports Americans Spent Largest Amount on Cosmetic Surgery Since the Great Recession of 2008," news release, March 20, 2014, http://www.surgery.org/media/news-releases/the-american-society-for-aesthetic-plastic-surgery-reports-americans-spent-largest-amount-on-cosmetic-surger.

4. Beth Moore, *Breaking Free: Making Liberty in Christ a Reality in Life* (Nashville: B&H Publishing Group, 2000), 238–42.

5. William Douglas-Home, *The Reluctant Debutante,* 1958 screenplay, adapted by Jenny Bicks and

Elizabeth Chandler, *What a Girl Wants*, Warner Bros., 2003.

Chapter 11: Confident Lady

1. Nancy Leigh DeMoss, *Lies Women Believe: And the Truth That Sets Them Free* (Chicago: Moody, 2006), 64.

Chapter 12: Forgiveness

1. Beth Moore, *Living Beyond Yourself: Exploring the Fruit of the Spirit* (Nashville: LifeWay Christian Resources, 2004), 127.

Chapter 14: In the World, Not of the World

1. Francis Chan, *Crazy Love: Overwhelmed by a Relentless God* (Colorado Springs: David C. Cook, 2008), 59.
2. Ibid., 91.

Chapter 15: Live Your Great Adventure

1. Francis Chan, "Fear God," *The Basic Series* video (Colorado Springs: David C. Cook, 2010), basicseries.com.

About the Author

LOVE, FAITH, AND FAMILY—these are important compo-
nents to understanding Lydia McLaughlin. While
her passion for life is evident to all who meet her, Lydia
is a grounded individual who is family oriented and business minded.

Lydia is a fan favorite from the hit Bravo TV show *The
Real Housewives of Orange County*. She is also managing
editor of *Beverly Hills Lifestyle* magazine.

The native Canadian now resides in Newport Beach,
California, where she manages three successful busi-
nesses, raises three young boys, keeps her marriage and
faith strong, and actively gives back to the community.

With a minor in theology, service as chaplain of her
sorority, and over fifteen years of leading women's groups,
Lydia has always had the desire to inspire.

WORTHY®
PUBLISHING

If you enjoyed this book, will you consider sharing the message with others?

- Mention the book in a Facebook post, Twitter update, Pinterest pin, blog post, or upload a picture through Instagram.
- Recommend this book to those in your small group, book club, workplace, and classes.
- Head over to facebook.com/worthypublishing, "LIKE" the page, and post a comment as to what you enjoyed the most.
- Tweet "I recommend reading #BeyondOrangeCounty by @OCLydia // @worthypub"
- Pick up a copy for someone you know who would be challenged and encouraged by this message.
- Write a book review online.

You can subscribe to Worthy Publishing's newsletter at worthypublishing.com.

WORTHY PUBLISHING
FACEBOOK PAGE

WORTHY PUBLISHING
WEBSITE